Counting of the OMER

A 49-Day Devotional

COUNTING OF THE OMER: A 49-Day Devotional on Psalm 119
Copyright © April 2025, Weiss Ministries, Inc.

All rights reserved. This book is protected by the copyright laws of the United States of America. No part of this devotional is to be photocopied, stored in a retrieval system, released into cyberspace, or
published without the expressed written permission of Weiss Ministries.

This devotional is based upon the Tree of Life Version
Copyright © 2015 by Messianic Jewish Family Bible Society
However, some Scriptural Quotations are taken from TLV, NIV, ESV, NASB, NKJV and AMP Bibles.

The Hebrew Name Yeshua is used instead of Jesus; other uses — G-D, ADONAI, ABBA, B'Shem Yeshua (In the Name of Yeshua), *Ruach HaKodesh* (Holy Spirit), EL SHADDAI, YHVH, LORD, Amain for Amen (in some cases)!

You may contact Weiss Ministries, Inc. at
www.weissministries.org
info@weissministries.org
touchinghisheart@gmail.com

1 2 3 4 5 6 7 8 9 10

ISBN: 9798317380632

Imprint: Independently published

Weiss Ministries, Inc.

Chesapeake, VA

Counting of the OMER

A 49-Day Devotional
on Psalm 119

by
JUANITA WEISS

WITH CONTRIBUTIONS FROM
NIA CASON
SARINA GILLILAND
JACKEE HERNDON
JILL JOHNSON
NELSON NORIEGA
CAROLE BUGLEWICZ POYSTI

USING THIS DEVOTIONAL

"Then you are to count from the morrow after the Shabbat, from the day that you brought the omer of the wave offering, seven complete Shabbatot. Until the morrow after the seventh Shabbat you are to count fifty days ..." (Leviticus 23:15-16).

It is a *mitzvah* (commandment) to Count the Omer (which was a measurement of barley), and to Count the Omer during its ordained time — from the beginning of *Chag HaMatzot* up to the Wheat Harvest at *Shavuot*!

The command is to count weeks and days. The Rabbis see this as two *mitzvot*. This devotional will facilitate your experience on this journey as we examine Psalm 119. The author is unnamed; older commentators almost universally said it is a psalm of David, composed throughout his entire life.

In this devotional, we will allude to the life of David as if this were so, even though he will be interchangeably referred to as "The Psalmist." Psalm 119 is arranged in an acrostic pattern. There are 22 letters in the Hebrew alphabet, and this psalm contains 22 units of 8 verses each. Each of the 22 sections is given a letter of the Hebrew alphabet, and each line in that section begins with that letter. The writers of this devotional may allude to the Hebrew letters in their reflection; some may not. However, the Hebrew letter is supplied on the intial page of each entry.

You are encouraged to write a reflection each day where space permits based upon what you glean from your meditation and reflection. May each day take you deeper into the Father's great love, His power, and reality. Thank you for joining us on this journey!

Happy Counting, My Friend.

COUNTING OF THE OMER — SEFIRAT HaOMER

During the Temple times, an elaborate ceremony developed of bringing an offering representing the earliest harvest, a sheaf of barley, as a thanksgiving tithe to G-D. During *Sefirat Ha'Omer*, the priest would meet the worshipers on the edge of the city and lead them up to the Temple mount with music, praise psalms, and dance.

On arriving at the Temple, the priest would take the sheaves of grain and lift some of them in the air, waving them in every direction, thus acknowledging God's provision and sovereignty over all the earth. (Kasdan, Barney, *God's Appointed Times*.) The traditional way to count the days during *Sefirat Ha'Omer* is by saying a certain prayer every evening and to mention the number of the current day of the omer. Use the following liturgy as you count the omer:

Chazzan (Leader)

Adonai blesses us with grace upon grace. Not only did He give us freedom and bring us out of Egypt, but He also gave us Torah. Not only did He give us Torah, but He also gave us Y'shua the Messiah. We count the omer starting on the second night of Passover, the Holy Day which recalls our freedom from Egypt. We end the counting of the Omer on Shavuot, a Holy Day in which we recall the giving of the Torah and also the outpouring of God's Spirit upon mankind.

All:

בָּרוּךְ אַתָּה
יְיָ אֱלֹהֵינוּ
מֶלֶךְ הָעוֹלָם
אֲשֶׁר קִדְּשָׁנוּ בְּמִצְוֹתָיו
וְצִוָּנוּ עַל סְפִירַת הָעֹמֶר:

Baruch ata Adonai, ELOHEYNU melech ha-olam, asher kiddeshanu bidvarecha v'tzi-va-noo al sifeerat ha-omer.

Blessed are you, O Adonai our God, King of the universe Who has sanctified us by your Word and commanded us concerning the counting of the omer.

Hayom Hazeh yom _____ *al sifeerat ha-omer.*
During the first week say, Today is day _____concerning the counting of the omer.

Through the rest of the weeks, say, "Today is day __ , which is __ week(s) and __ day(s) of the Omer."

Chazzan (Leader)
It was in faith that our fathers brought an omer of barley to the Temple. This firstfruit from the harvest was an act of faith that Adonai would provide the rest of the harvest. It is by faith that we believe Y'shua of Nazareth to be the firstfruits of the resurrection. We know that since Adonai has raised Y'shua from the grave, then we too will be resurrected to everlasting life in the last days.

All:
"I tell you that unless a singular grain of wheat that falls to the ground dies, it stays just a grain; but if it dies, it produces a huge harvest" (John 12:24)

For Messianic believers, the purpose of the counting goes beyond the agricultural significance. This feast points us to the resurrection of Messiah. It is a harvest festival where the grain that came from the earth is lifted high for all to see.

Blessed are you, Adonai our God! Thank you for allowing us to see this season of the Counting of the Omer. May Messiah be lifted high in our lives and in this world for all to see. May we see a harvest of souls of both Jews and nonJews during this season as we celebrate the Bread from Heaven and expect supernatural encounters with You. In Yeshua's Name. Amen.

Sefirat HaOmer is the time when the Israelites crossed the Sea and sojourned at the base of Mt. Sinai. It is also the time when Ruth and Naomi returned to Bethlehem Judah, and when Yeshua, after His resurrection, showed many infallible proofs that He was the Messiah. What else could occur on these days?!

GLOSSARY

Below are the words used in Psalm 119 that refer to the "Word of G-D":

- **Law** (*torah*, used 25 times): "Its parent vb means 'teach' or 'direct'; therefore coming from G-d it means both 'law' and 'revelation.' It can be used of a single command or of a whole body of law." (Derek Kidner)
- **Word** (*dabar*, used 24 times): The idea is of the spoken word, God's revealed word to man. 'Proceeding from his mouth and revealed by him to us...'" (Matthew Poole)
- **Judgments** (*mishpatim*, used 23 times): "...from *shaphat*, to judge, determine, regulate, order, and discern, because they judge concerning our words and works; show the rules by which they should be regulated; and cause us to discern what is right and wrong, and decide accordingly." (Adam Clarke)
- **Testimonies** (*edut/edot*, 23 times): This word is related to the word for witness. To obey His testimonies "signifies loyalty to the terms of the covenant made between the Lord and Israel." (Willem VanGemeren)
- **Commandments** (*mitzvah/mitzuot*, used 22 times): "This word emphasizes the straight authority of what is said... the right to give orders." (Derek Kidner)
- **Statutes** (*bukkim*, used 21 times): The noun is derived from the root verb 'engrave' or 'inscribe'; the idea is the written word of G-D and the authority of His written word:
" ...declaring his authority and power of giving us laws." (Matthew Poole)

- **Precepts** (*piqqudim*, used 21 times): "This is a word drawn from the sphere of an officer or overseer, a man who is responsible to look closely into a situation and take action.... So the word points to the particular instructions of the Lord, as of one who cares about detail."(Derek Kidner)
- **Word** (*imrah*, used 19 times): "*Imrah* is similar in meaning to *dabar*, yet a different term. The 'word' may denote anything G-D has spoken, commanded, or promised." (Willem VanGemeren)
https://enduringword.com/bible-commentary/psalm-119/

1 – COUNTING THE OMER א

"Today is Day 1 Concerning the Counting of the Omer."

Blessed are those whose way is blameless, who walk in the Torah of Adonai. Happy are those who keep His testimonies, who seek Him with a whole heart, who also do no injustice, but walk in His ways (1-3).

Psalm 119 begins with the letter *aleph* (א) (which can mean 'champion'), and it is the first letter of the word *ashrey*/אשרי which begins this psalm. A*shrey*/אשרי can mean "happy, blessed, fortunate, joyful." Actually, it means all of those concepts and so much more because, as you can see, not one English word is adequate enough to explain the Hebrew concept of *ashrey*/אשרי. The Hebrew word means something like "deeply contented." The DHE says *ashrey*/אשרי should be rendered, *"Oh, the gladness of."* I absolutely love what theologian William Barclay said: "…it is that Joy which has its secret within itself, that joy which is serene and untouchable, and self-contained, that Joy which is completely independent of all the chances and changes of life."

And I say, "It is a state or condition of having absolute confidence in G-D that the external stimuli do not affect your state! The external conditions are actually affected by your posture, your lifestyle, and your mindset because of *ashrey* / אשרי!" Your *ashrey* / אשרי gets to impact that which is external! Imagine that!

Do those conditions change? Maybe not! But your perception of them do, which will make all the difference in the world!

David, assuming he is the psalmist in Psalm 119, said that a person is *ashrey /* אשרי if his/her ways are blameless! How can that be? "I made an error today," you might say! "I sinned! Just like David, my life is not squeaky clean!"

But I've got some questions for you: Are you lost in Him? Have you sought repentance? Have you realized the severity of breaking His heart? If you are and have, then you walk in the way of the Lord! His ways were all about bringing us to Himself! If you have been brought to Him and seek to bring others to him, then, my friend, you *are* blameless! *Ashrey /* אשרי*!*

Here's the kicker! Another *ashrey* moment—keeping *a'do'tav/* עדתיו) *"His testimonies"*! This implies that you know what He values and that you value that yourself! It means that you guard those things that testify of Him like a changed life and a life full of *mitzvot*, good deeds! It means finding His footsteps and walking in them! Doing what He does! Making His ways your own!

When He sees us doing that, then, in His eyes, we have done no wrong.

That, my friend, is *Ashrey /* אשרי*!!!!*

That is champion!

O, the gladness of the one who has done no wrong in His eyes. Oh the Blessed state of the one who walks in His ways!

DECLARE THESE WORDS TODAY: *Ashrey! Thriving! Shavuot/ Pentecost!*

Notes / Prayers / Reflections / Revelations

_____

_____

_____

_____

2 – COUNTING THE OMER א

"Today is Day 2 Concerning the Counting of the Omer."

You have commanded that Your precepts be kept diligently. Oh that my ways were steadfast to observe Your decrees! (4-5).

Father wants us to keep His precepts, His *pi'ku'dim / פקודים*! If we fail to keep them, they are *still* His statutes! They are *"forever settled in heavens"* according to Psalm 119:89! The Father's desire is that we would keep them for our own good. Moses says at one point that these words, the words of Torah, they are our life (Deuteronomy 32:47)! So why would He NOT want us to partake of that which is really life, really living? Apart from following His precepts, diligently keeping them, we are merely existing. But when we walk in that which is our life... we thrive!

During the reign of King Josiah of Judah in 2 Kings 22, a Torah scroll was discovered when they were renovating the Temple. When He realized the *piqu'dim / פקודים* it contained, he quickly re-instituted the reading of the Torah and brought about reform by getting rid of idols and idolatry. He realized that the key to their existence was in the Torah, and the Torah promoted the worship of the one true G-D, the only G-D.

Beloved, I beseech you as David did, G-D has designed that His Word be kept diligently for the sake of our families, our nation, this world, for the sake of the coming redemption. Diligently is "characterized by steady, earnest, and energetic effort." We must put forth the effort to read and keep His *piqu'dim* / פקודים. They must never become lost to us.

David's only lament in this section is that as he is walking the straight and narrow way that he *might* forget the precepts of the Lord. All he wanted more than anything was to be more steadfast, more faithful, more earnest, enduring and energetic so that he would be able to keep the decrees that HaShem so longs that all of us would keep.

Beloved, you are at an added advantage. You see what David went through. This does not have to be your lot! You can be steadfast! You can adhere to the precepts! You can be faithful!

- You can do everything He's charged you to do (Phil. 4:13).
- You have the *Ruach HaKodesh* as your Helper (John 14:26-28)!
- You have the finished work of Yeshua! (Romans 5:9)!
- My Point ... keep His commandments! Be steadfast and thrive!

DECLARE THESE WORDS TODAY: *Persevering! Thriving! ShavuotPentecost!*

Notes / Prayers / Reflections / Revelations

_____
_____
_____
_____
_____
_____
_____
_____

3 – COUNTING THE OMER א

"Today is Day 3 Concerning the Counting of the Omer."

I will praise You with an upright heart as I learn Your righteous judgments. I will observe Your statutes. Never abandon me utterly!" (7-8).

Do me a favor! Pick your favorite verse out of the Bible! Recite it! Meditate on it! Let its morsels of pure truth get caught between your teeth; let it pique the tastebuds and then slide down your throat! That was what the Word of G-D was like to the Psalmist. He calls the Word "judgments" and "statutes"! He knows that if he could just "learn" them, then he would be able to give G-D praise with an upright heart! That's what it is all about, isn't it?!

I have found that the more I know about G-D and His Word, the easier it is for me to praise Him! His judgments and His precepts are who He is. As we worship and praise Him, we can get a hold of the reality that the Psalmist longed for. He did not want G-D to abandon him utterly.

In my study of The Sermon on the Mount, there is something that Yeshua says that is always so penetrating. He says, "Many will say to Me on that day, 'Lord, Lord, didn't we prophesy in Your name, and drive out demons in Your name, and perform many miracles in Your name?'" (Matthew 7:22). His response will be "I never knew you. Get away from Me, you workers of lawlessness!" *That*, Beloved, is utter abandonment — to be departed from the G-D of Love — never to be able to draw near to Him again.

What does that look like? Really I do not want to know, but Yeshua gives us a sense of what that is like. He says where the wicked are, *"There will be weeping there, and gnashing of teeth…"* (Luke 13:28) and there will be *"outer darkness"* (Matthew 8:12). That's what the state of "utter abandonment" looks like.

So in the midst of our "Lord, Lord's," and in the midst of our doing miracles, and operating in what we call spiritual gifts, we could be consequentially abandoned by G-D as a result of our heart motivations.

So David knows the secret of staying in G-D's favor. It is staying in the Word. If we keep it in our hearts; if we let those words become who we are, it is only *then* that we have the assurance that the Heavenly Father will not abandon us... never *ever* … and especially not *utterly*.

DECLARE THESE WORDS TODAY: *Never Abandoned! Shavuot/Pentecost! 46MoreDaysLeft!*

Notes / Prayers / Reflections / Revelations

_____

_____

_____

_____

_____

_____

_____

_____

4 – COUNTING THE OMER   ב

"Today is Day 4 Concerning the Counting of the Omer."

"How can a young man keep his way pure? By guarding it according to Your word. With my whole heart have I sought You — let me not stray from Your mitzvot" (9-10).

    As we enter into the section *bet* (ב) of Psalm 119, let's think about implications of the heading. The symbol of the Hebrew letter *bet* (ב) is a "house." "House" in Hebrew is the word *beit*/בית; as you can see it is spelled with a *bet* (ב). Additionally as a word, *bet* (ב) means "in." Do we want our homes to be a place of purity, creating an atmosphere for the presence of HaShem to live "in" as we live lives of wholeness in accordance with HaShem's commands? Do we want the "in"-bringing of more life and G-Dliness into our lives individually and our families corporately?

    We often think of the home as being our ultimate comfort zone, a place where we can let our hair down and relax. This scripture pairs beautifully with its heading, such that to really relax and be "in" shalom with G-D and man, we must have hearts which seek after G-D. It also means that we have a deep desire to keep our walk guarded and pure before Him.

    Romans 12:18 points out the importance of living in peace with everyone as much as possible; this fits beautifully with Galatians 5:22-23 where we see the "Fruit of the Spirit" outlined? *"But the fruit of the Ruach is love, joy, peace, patience, kindness, goodness, faithfulness, gentleness, and self-control-against such things there is no law."* I encourage you to review and meditate on these fruit, how each one builds upon the another, steering us in the direction of purity, whether we are young in age, faith, or in challenged areas.

What an important image this creates as we live out His fruit so we can walk in purity with our whole heart. This in turn will help us to be steadfast in His *mitzvot*... line upon line, precept upon precept!

The psalmist asks HaShem to help him not to stray. He isn't asking to be harnessed against his will, but he is surrendering his will to the will of HaShem. We, too, can harness ourselves and surrender our wills to Him with our whole heart! Let's purpose to do that as we count up!!

REFLECTION: What emotional "home-base" do you find yourself "in"? Is it grounded "in" things above, though you live and function on this earth? This emotional and spiritual positioning will contribute to where your "WHOLE" heart will be focused... if it is in conflict, it will not function fully "whole."

DECLARE THESE WORDS TODAY: *Never Abandoned! Shavuot/Pentecost! 46MoreDaysLeft!*

Notes / Prayers / Reflections / Revelations

_____

_____

_____

_____

_____

5 – COUNTING THE OMER ב

"Today is Day 5 Concerning the Counting of the Omer."

"With my lips I rehearse all the rulings of Your mouth. I rejoice in the way of Your testimonies above all wealth. I will meditate on Your precepts, and regard Your ways. I will delight in Your decrees. I will never forget Your word" (13-16).

In the second half of *bet* (ב), it, in many ways, brings Day 5 full circle. Much of what we walk out in love, joy, peace, long suffering, gentleness, goodness, faithfulness and temperance is demonstrated with our lips, or the tongue. We know from James 3:6, *"So also the tongue is a small member-yet it boasts of great things. See how so small a fire sets a blaze so great a forest!"* WOW! That's some kind of power! Verse 13 says we are to rehearse the rulings of HIS mouth, not our own... not our own rulings or our judgements...Eeekkk! If we take on His responsibility of Judge, then we have to carry the rest of His duties. We all can agree that's above our "pay grade" for certain.

Can we be fruit inspectors and pray for insight for His *Ruach HaKodesh* to lead us in what we speak? Yes, as He leads, speaking His truth in love is powerful, and we pray His desired effect will result in His glory and honor. The keys are His precepts and ways from which we carefully speak His truth, in His love. May He bathe us all "in/ב" His grace also knowing the responsibility for response belongs to the hearer; we are all to be obedient.

Verse 14 equates "wealth" with the value of His testimony. Luke 6:45 exhorts, *"Out of the good treasure of his heart the good man brings forth good, and out of evil the evil man brings forth evil. For from the overflow of the heart his mouth speaks."* As we know only HaShem can lead us to bring forth wealth which is non-perishable and eternal in holiness. These words should not only be good, but they should come forth grounded in Him, His intention and truth. These are characteristics of Yeshua we are to meditate on and apply to our household *bet* (ב) and our ways.

REFLECTION: Let's take this a step farther... as we build our household with Him, where is HIS household? YES, IN US!! We are His holy habitation from which we can delight in Him, His decrees, His Word!! It's reciprocal! We are NEVER to forget them and no matter what, HE will NEVER forget us!! What a place of peace and rest He affords us to dwell in and live from as HE LIVES IN US! Selah!

DECLARE THESE WORDS TODAY: *His Rulings! His Grace! Dwelling!*

Notes / Prayers / Reflections / Revelations

_____

_____

_____

_____

_____

_____

_____

6 – COUNTING THE OMER ג

"Today is Day 6 Concerning the Counting of the Omer."

"Do good to your servant, that I may live and keep your word. Open my eyes, so I may behold wonders from Your Torah. I am a temporary dweller on earth - do not hide your mitzvot from me" (17-19).

When you read these verses, you can imagine the love the Psalmist had for Torah and his G-D! Pray these prayers with me, that we too might emulate His passion for holiness.

Oh, the nourishment of Your presence! Come commune with me, Abba! As You gift me with a new day, I open my eyes to Your goodness and favor. I have yet to behold all the deep rich flavors of the Torah. I am hungry, even ravenous, for every crumb of wisdom and revelation You have placed for me to see and run with. I only have a short time here on this earth to sit with You and feast on the wonders of Your Word. Yet, temporary as I am, how amazing that You want nothing more than to commune with me and watch as I taste every jot and every tittle of Your amazing banquet called Torah.

As you pray this prayer, be reminded of others who were ravenous for His Word. Remember Lazarus! Martha! And we cannot forget her sister Miriam, who was so drawn away from the mundane cooking and cares of the house to join the men sitting at Yeshua's feet. I can imagine that her eyes were transfixed upon His visage. I believe her ears were perked, waiting for Him to emit every syllable of the timeless words He spoke. And as she listened, she became more than *"a temporary dweller on the earth."* I believe she had transcended time and space in order to feast on the other-worldliness of His words. He was speaking of heavenly things, of the Kingdom, of the Father who had sent Him. He was not hiding His Word from her. She knew that not one morsel of the Bread of Life would fall from His lips without her catching it. Solomon says, *"Wisdom has built her house. ... she has also set her table"* (Proverbs 9:1-2). But wisdom will not make you eat. Wisdom will remind you to withdraw to the table, but it will not make you sit.

On this 6th day, would you, too, become more than a *"temporary dweller of the earth"* and FEAST on Words of a Kingdom that *is*... and also that which is to Come!

DECLARE THESE WORDS TODAY: *Nourishment! Feasting! Counting Up! Shavuot/Pentecost!*

Notes / Prayers / Reflections / Revelations

_____

_____

_____

_____

_____

_____

_____

7 – COUNTING THE OMER ג

"Today is Day 7, which is 1 Week and 0 Days of the Omer."

My soul is crushed with longing for your judgements at all times. You rebuke the proud, who are cursed, who wander from your mitzvot. Take scorn and contempt away from me, for I have kept your testimonies (20-22).

I do want You to mold me and shape me. As Your clay, I long to feel the hands that will shape my tomorrow and direct me. Discipline me and keep me focused so that I will keep Your commandments and not wrestle with my unruly heart, mind and soul. You have kept me and taught me Your ordinances so that I, with authority, will speak to my heart and remove its proud demeanor. I give my heart permission to be tested and cleansed in Your hands. I must remove my will and allow Yours to lead. Your opinion of me is the only one that matters.

Though princes sit and talk against me, Your servant meditates on your decrees. For your testimonies are my delight - they are also my counselors. (23-24)

There comes a point in my walk with You, ABBA, when I cease to hear the vain prattle of the enemy. I run eagerly into the beauty and strength of Your laws and the embrace of Your Son, Yeshua. I am understanding the Way, Truth and Life of Your testimonies. These three are my teachers: Father, Son, Ruach. I have been so hungry for so long and the aroma of Your Word and the deliciousness of Your Spirit complete my very existence. I am full and free to adorn You with praises. These praises, You do not need from me, but You delight in my surrender to Your Majesty.

David has given us the answer to slander, to persecution, and anything else the enemy throws our way. He says that we are never left without a counselor. It is very interesting that when Yeshua says He has to go away that He would send "another" counselor. It's not "another"... different, but "another" the same. Just as we cannot separate the *Ruach HaKodesh* from Yeshua, neither can we separate the Torah from Him as well. David says, *"Your Word, O Lord, has been my Counselor."* May His Word be yours as well!

DECLARE THESE WORDS TODAY: *The Answer To Adversity! Counting UP! Shavuot! TORAH!*

Notes / Prayers / Reflections / Revelations

_____

_____

_____

_____

_____

_____

_____

_____

_____

_____

9 – COUNTING THE OMER ד

"Today is Day 9, which is 1 Week and 2 Days of the Omer."

Turn me away from the deceitful way, and be gracious to me with Your Torah. I have chosen the way of faithfulness. I have set my heart on Your judgments. I cling to Your testimonies. Adonai, do not put me to shame! I run the course of Your mitzvot, for You open wide my heart (29-32).

It takes humility to repent and surrender to walk from our selfish human nature through the "door" / דלת of awareness as HaShem envisions for you so that you can truthfully ... live. He says in Revelation 3:20, *"Behold, I stand at the door and knock. If anyone hears My voice and opens the door, I will come in to him and will dine with him, and he with Me."* The door which we choose to walk through will determine where we sit in the future as verse 21 says, *"To the one who overcomes I will grant the right to sit with Me on My throne, just as I myself overcame and sat down with My Father on His throne."* We must hear and surrender as in verse 22, *"He who has an ear, let him hear what the Ruach is saying to Messiah's communities."* We don't want to be shamed; this requires a contrite heart and constant surrendering to HaShem's ways, His Torah, and His judgements.

Verse 29b holds a very precious perspective HaShem wants us to have: His Torah as a source of His graciousness. It's much more than lots of stories with rules! Throughout the Torah, HaShem is showing us His path to redemption; how to live in a condition of being forgiven; to be

8 – COUNTING THE OMER ד

"Today is Day 8, which is 1 Week and 1 Day of the Omer."

My soul clings to the dust. Revive me according to Your word! I told of my ways and You answered me. Teach me Your statutes. Help me discern the way of Your precepts, so I may meditate on Your wonders. My soul weeps with grief. Make me stand firm with Your word (25-28).

As we enter section *dalet* (ד) in Psalm 119, we must take notice that *dalet* (ד) literally means "door"/ דלת in Hebrew and is symbolized by a door, a path or a way of life. In today's verses we see the expression of one having fallen below HaShem's statutes, and through repentance, crying for help. What a real and beautiful example of taking the "door" of humility available to us all, desiring to live out of who HaShem says He is and how and upon what He can firmly stand. King David is asking for Torah, and he craves discernment of what was imparted to Moses to the extent that his mind, will and emotions are grievously weeping.

This is reminiscent of how we are given the *Ruach HaKodesh* Who can intercede as in Romans 8:26-27: *"In the same way, the Ruach helps in our weakness. For we do not know how to pray as we should, but the Ruach Himself intercedes for us with groans too deep for words. And He who searches the hearts knows the mind of the Ruach, because He intercedes for the kedoshim according to the will of God."* Could this level of engagement with HaShem be utilizing a "door" for His supernatural goodness and presence to rise up in us greater than any other, thus enabling us to stand? Most assuredly yes, and even at our greatest time of weakness. HalleluYah!

We came from the dust of the earth and from the dust we will return. When David says his soul clings to the dust, whether before life or after, this is when we are void of free-will. But what our author is doing is surrendering his free will so he may meditate on G-D's wonders. The author wants to stand firm on HaShem's Word, not his own. This is analogous with, *"Thy will be done on earth as it is in Heaven"* (Matthew 6:10). It is a demonstration of absolute humility to relinquish all... just as Yeshua willingly did for us all not only on the tree, but also in the entirety of His steps "on earth" as it was His/our Father's will in Heaven.

Oh, that we always do the same!

DECLARE THESE WORDS TODAY: *The Door of Humility! Counting UP! Shavuot! Pentecost!*

Notes / Prayers / Reflections / Revelations

_____
_____
_____
_____
_____
_____
_____
_____
_____
_____

9 – COUNTING THE OMER ת

"Today is Day 9, which is 1 Week and 2 Days of the Omer."

Turn me away from the deceitful way, and be gracious to me with Your Torah. I have chosen the way of faithfulness. I have set my heart on Your judgments. I cling to Your testimonies. Adonai, do not put me to shame! I run the course of Your mitzvot, for You open wide my heart (29-32).

It takes humility to repent and surrender to walk from our selfish human nature through the "door" / דלת of awareness as HaShem envisions for you so that you can truthfully ... live. He says in Revelation 3:20, *"Behold, I stand at the door and knock. If anyone hears My voice and opens the door, I will come in to him and will dine with him, and he with Me."* The door which we choose to walk through will determine where we sit in the future as verse 21 says, *"To the one who overcomes I will grant the right to sit with Me on My throne, just as I myself overcame and sat down with My Father on His throne."* We must hear and surrender as in verse 22, *"He who has an ear, let him hear what the Ruach is saying to Messiah's communities."* We don't want to be shamed; this requires a contrite heart and constant surrendering to HaShem's ways, His Torah, and His judgements.

Verse 29b holds a very precious perspective HaShem wants us to have: His Torah as a source of His graciousness. It's much more than lots of stories with rules! Throughout the Torah, HaShem is showing us His path to redemption; how to live in a condition of being forgiven; to be ultimately fulfilled through Yeshua; how to walk in faith; and where to set our hearts. Just think, David's heart before Yeshua had to be "open wide" to fulfill HaShem's *mitzvot*.

And today we have His Word; the fulfillment of Israel becoming a nation again; enlivening of the Bride through Yeshua, the ultimate sacrifice once and for all; and the constant indwelling of His *Ruach HaKodesh* - how much can we trust Him with our hearts "open wide" and ready to obey? We have the *Brit Chadasha* to further guide and enunciate the fulfillment of the Torah and Tanach. What a blessed time in which we live!

REFLECTION: When you sense the precious, holy "knock" on the door of your heart, you have the choice to open the door. I exhort you to enact your freewill and say, "*Here I am*/הנני." Petition Him as our author demonstrated with your heart *"open wide."*

DECLARE THESE WORDS TODAY: *The Door of Humility! Counting UP! Shavuot! Pentecost!*

Notes / Prayers / Reflections / Revelations

_____

_____

_____

_____

_____

_____

_____

10 – COUNTING THE OMER ה

"Today is Day 10, which is 1 Week and 3 Days of the Omer."

Teach me the way of Your decrees, Adonai, and I will follow them to the end. Give me understanding, that I may keep Your Torah and observe it with all my heart. Help me walk in the path of Your mitzvot - for I delight in it. Turn my heart to Your testimonies and not to dishonest gain (33-36).

    Riding in my friend's car down Santa Monica Boulevard was terrifying. Every red light came as a surprise to her as she slammed on the brakes just shy of the car in front of us. At the green light, she gunnned it, switched lanes, and raced to the next red light before slamming brakes again. To my knowledge, she has never gotten a ticket or been in an accident. On paper, you would say she's an excellent driver. In practicum, she's a horrible driver. She follows the "rules" technically, but the way she follows them is painful for her passengers.
    David requests HaShem to teach him the way (*derech* / דרך / "manner") of His decrees, or "prescribed tasks" so that he can follow them to the end. Why not just learn the tasks and get on with it, like ironing, or tax returns? Because, like my friend, it's not the keeping of the law that impresses HaShem or "gives us a smooth ride"; it's the manner in which we keep it. David is a man after G-D's own heart because he asks for the understanding so that Torah is not a burden! His wife may have disapproved of the "way" he brought the Ark up to Jerusalem, but he's ALL IN once he learns the rules of conduct.

With his whole heart, whole being, or *"etsem,"* which also means "essence," He obeys. The "essence" of the Torah is what G-D is looking for in us. Is it dancing out of my delighted heart, or am I a judgmental "good girl" following rules?

The essence of every prescribed task that Yeshua fulfilled was *Chesed* (Loving-Kindness). Whether praying, feeding, healing, forgiving, rebuking, suffering, or dying, His motive was compassion.

It fueled Him.

Whatever *mitzvah* we perform, if we aren't "all in" with *Chesed*, I doubt we'll stay motivated to "The End" as the "love of most grows cold" and we experience persecution. If we don't love the manner of His Word today, we will abandon "rules" quickly.

Yeshua! Infuse us with Loving-Kindness as we keep your Word, so that we will be able to keep it to the end!

DECLARE THESE WORDS TODAY: *ALL in! Until the End! Counting Up! Pentecost/Shavuot!*

Notes / Prayers / Reflections / Revelations

11 – COUNTING THE OMER ה

"Today is Day 11, which is 1 Week and 4 Days of the Omer."

Turn my eyes away from gazing at vanity but revive me in Your ways. Fulfill Your word to Your servant, which leads to reverence for You. Make the disgrace I dread pass away for Your judgements are good. Behold, I long for Your precepts. Revive me by Your righteousness (37-40).

Gazing for hours at the cover of *TV Guide* featuring David Cassidy, my eight-year-old heart longed to marry him. OK, yes, I would even smack little kisses, and my brothers would tease me about it for decades. Well, I never did meet, let alone marry, David, with nary a regret over his unrequited love. But it took nearly 40 years of wandering in the desert of romantic oblivion before I would lock eyes with my friend, Charlie, vowing to embrace a new life together as one.

When I glance at an object, whether a kitty in a pet store, a couch, a necklace, an animal meme on FaceBook, a fear-based YouTube video; if my eyes linger for more than a second (I'm sure there are studies on this), my mind starts processing how to acquire it, ingest it or act on it. A small percentage of it may offer benefit to my spiritual life, but the rest is distraction, or worse, temptation to lust, fear, envy, or rage.

Is it any wonder we're assaulted by advertisements and emotional manipulations? Arguably, every one of the Ten Words warn of the desperation for something or someone else to fulfill us.

The first word of verses 37 and 39 is *a-var* / עבר which means "to cross over." Add a "yod" (י) to the end of this root and you get *iv-ri* / עברי or "Hebrew" which, of course, at its core, means "the one who crossed over, passed through."

Twice in these four verses we find the word "היני / *ha'ye'ni*" ("make me alive") as the antidote to time wasted on what our deceitful little heart convinces us will make us whole. The psalmist David, writer of the psalm and thus the verses above, dreads the disgrace of false hope and has surmised the only way through is on the Life-boat of Adonai's righteousness and essence.

Author and Fulfiller of deepest longings, help us pass over worthless idols. As we gaze at Your glory, quicken our hearts to linger only with You.

"You have stolen my heart, my sister, my bride; you have stolen my heart with one glance of your eyes, with one jewel of your necklace" (Song of Songs 4:9).

Yeshua, may I be Your distraction.

DECLARE THESE WORDS TODAY: *Crossing Over! Upon You I Linger! Shavuot-Pentecost!*

Notes / Prayers / Reflections / Revelations

_____

_____

_____

_____

_____

_____

_____

12 – COUNTING THE OMER ו

"Today is Day 12, which is 1 Week and 5 Days of the Omer."

May Your lovingkindnesses come to me, Adonai — Your salvation according to Your word—so I may answer the one taunting me, for I trust in Your word (41-42).

The word translated as "loving kindness" is *chesed*/ חסד. It can mean any of these words: mercy (149x), kindness (40x), lovingkindness (30x), goodness (12x), kindly (5x), merciful (4x), favour (3x), good (1x), goodliness (1x), pity. Notice the number of times it is used in the *Tanach* (OT).

David prays that the *chesed* / חסד of Adonai would come to him. I believe that this plea is akin to the cry, "Have mercy upon me." When the blind man in Mark 10:47, who was sitting on the road to Jericho, heard that Yeshua was passing by, this is what he cried: *"Yeshua, Son of David, have mercy on me!"* When everyone wanted him to be quiet, Yeshua stopped His ascent into Jerusalem and asked the man, *"What do you want Me to do for you?"* I find that "Have Mercy" is a prayer the the LORD always answers! His mercies are purposeful! It was not just the result of Adam's and Chavah's disobedience that drove them from the Garden; it was the mercies of G-D! What if they had eaten of the Tree of Life and lived forever in their fallen state?

Thus, the mercies of G-D may not always look like what we imagine!

The Psalmist also requests that the salvation, *t'shu'ah* / תשועה, that's based upon G-D's Word, also be assigned to him. The taunting of the enemy must have been a major onslaught in David's life that he pleads for both *chesed / חסד* and *t'shu'ah / תשועה*. It is interesting to note that this salvation is deliverance (usually by G-D through a human vessel). I know you are like me when I say that however the LORD sends His salvation, it will always be for our good! David knows that the salvation promised in the Word of G-D is true, tested and tried! We see its evidence in the pages of Biblical Scripture.

May we, like David, trust in G-D's Word! May it be our go-to as well! Salvation according to the Word! That is how you answer everything—according to the Word!

Yeshua in Matthew 4:4 answered the adversary, the one taunting Him, with the Word! He declares, *"Man shall not live by bread alone, but by every word that comes from the mouth of God."*

May the power and truth of the Word of GOD be our trust!

DECLARE THESE WORDS TODAY: *Have Mercy! Chesed! Trusting His Word! Pentecost!*

Notes / Prayers / Reflections / Revelations

13 – COUNTING THE OMER 1

"Today is Day 13, which is 1 Week and 6 Days of the Omer."

Never snatch out of my mouth a word of truth, for I hope in Your judgments. So I may always keep Your Torah, forever and ever, and walk about in freedom. For I have sought Your precepts (43-45).

Yeshua tells a story of a man who sows seeds in Matthew 4. He says that the kingdom of heaven is just like that — a man sowing seeds. This man sows seeds on rocky ground; the birds of the air come and eat of the seeds because there was no place for the seeds to embed themselves. Yeshua says that the seed is the Word, and that the bird is hasatan who comes to take from us the very word that is sown into us. Here the Psalmist is asking G-D never to snatch out of his mouth a word of truth. I know that this is David's plea to the degree that he did not want to miss anything that G-D would speak to him. Not only did he not want to miss it, but he prayed that the Word would never depart from him.

David acknowledges HaShem's complete sovereignty. He is indeed sovereign over the fish of the sea, the fowl of the air and the beasts of the field. And so David seems to be praying what we find in the Disciples Prayer: *"Lead me not into temptation but deliver me from evil"* (Matthew 6:13). What a prayer to indeed pray to Hashem: never snatch any word of truth from our lips, thus allowing them to flow into our very hearts and souls, lodge themselves there and take root. In this way, David gets to keep Torah forever and ever.

In order to keep it, it must find a lodging place, unlike the seeds sown on rocky ground, and that lodging place is the fertile soil of the heart made malleable to His massaging touch.

And David knows what we need to know, that keeping the words of Torah is not burdensome; it's freedom, liberating! For too long we have been told that Torah is legalistic and suffocating and obsolete. Paul says this so beautifully in Rom. 13:8: *"Let no debt remain outstanding, except the continuing debt to love one another, for whoever loves others has fulfilled the law."* There is such freedom in the Father's love.

So, Beloved, let's seek the precepts of Torah so that we, too, can walk in freedom and realize that Hashem wants His Word hidden in our hearts ... for He is sovereign, over the giving of His Word, the work of His Word and its preservation! Halleluyah and Amen!

DECLARE THESE WORDS TODAY: *Torah Is Freedom! The Word-the Seed-theHeart! Counting Up!*

Notes / Prayers / Reflections / Revelations

14 – COUNTING THE OMER ו

"Today is Day 14, which is 2 Weeks and 0 Days of the Omer."

I will speak of Your testimonies before kings, and never be ashamed. I delight in Your mitzvot, which I love. I reach out my hands for Your mitzvot, which I love, and meditate on Your decrees (46-48).

Did David really know the importance the *mitzvot*, the commandments given by G-D? Did he know that at the end of the age that the Bride would be dressed in *mitzvot*, her righteous deeds, according to Rev. 19:8—"*She was given fine linen to wear, bright and clean! For the fine linen is the righteous deeds of the kedoshim.*" Did he know that Yeshua the Messiah would say, *"...let your light shine before men so they may see your good works and glorify your Father in heaven"* (Matthew 5:16)? If he didn't know about the last two, he knew how important the *mitzvot* were that they had become his delight, something in which he could "take pleasure"!

What do you delight in? The next movie you'll binge-watch? That succulent steak dinner, cooked to perfection? Your marriage? Your job? Your children?

David's delight was in G-D's commandments. He says he loves them. What I'm about to say you, you'll probably read at least ten times or more in this devotional. Here it is: G-D's commandments are not grievous or burdensome (1 John 5:3). We attempt to make them so, but they are not! They should be the source of our delight and affections.

David continues by saying he reaches our his hands for the *mitzvot*, to do them.

For example, when Yeshua said, *"Blessed are the peacemakers"* (Matthew 5:9), He meant that you should not just "be" *at* peace, but you should *make* peace. Where there is discord, you are the one who should bring peace — to the point of surrendering your rights to bring it about.

Consider this: David had every right to take the life of King Saul who was trying to kill him, but he didn't do it, even though he had several opportunities. He reached our his hand to do a *mitzvah*, instead! In this way, he had no shame in presenting the testimonies of G-D before Kings.

Say with me: **Father, may I get to the place of loving your *mitzvot*, of delighting in them, reaching out my hands actively to do them, and not to be ashamed of them... even in the face of those who have high positións. Amen!**

DECLARE THESE WORDS TODAY: *Mitzvot! The Dress of the Bride! MyDelight! Shavuot!*

Notes / Prayers / Reflections / Revelations

_____

_____

_____

_____

_____

_____

_____

_____

15 – COUNTING THE OMER ט

"Today is Day 15, which is 2 Weeks and 1 Day of the Omer."

Remember the word to Your servant, on which You have made me hope. My comfort in affliction is this: Your word has kept me alive (49-50).

I love little kids. The one thing that bugs me about them, though, is their memory, especially as it pertains to the slightest suggestion, let alone promise, I may have uttered. A kid can hold us like political prisoners of guilt with two simple words: "You said." Adonai doesn't need reminding, but I suspect He hopes that His children will point to His written promises and declare, "You said!" By doing so it shows that we're not only paying attention, but also we expect Him to be trustworthy! To not complete a word spoken is *anathema* to the pure in heart. Recall the Simple Child of the Seder, who asks a basic question about *Pesach* and expects a straightforward answer.

The arrogant or sarcastic child (The Wicked Child of the Seder) sows seeds of doubt and mistrust. Perhaps she or he has had her/ his hopes dashed too many times because of misplaced trust. Unfortunately, this child finds comfort in mocking the innocence of the child who trusts in the goodness and reliability of Adonai.

But True Comfort, as we know from verses 50 and 52, comes only from the Word of Adonai - the Faithful and True. It is the Mature Child, regardless of affliction or ridicule, who habitually remembers (*zakar*/זכר) and waits in patient expectation for Him to make good His promise. We are, then, weaned from the false comforts derived from anything, or anyone else.

It is no surprise to me that the seventh letter of the Hebrew Aleph-Bet is the *zayin* (ז), which means "sword" or "scythe." By the Sword of the Spirit, The Word of Adonai, we will see every oath ("sheva" שבע - "seven") fulfilled.

Adonai, we take up Your promises and judgements in Your Word, as our sword and our scythe. We declare today that we are the Workers of the Harvest that Messiah Yeshua admonished His *talmidim* to pray for. We will find strength in no other weapon; we will find comfort in no other god. Your Word is True and we trust only You. YOU are my Comfort in affliction!!!

DECLARE THESE WORDS TODAY: *True Comfort! Sword of the Spirit! ShavuotPentecost!*

Notes / Prayers / Reflections / Revelations

16 – COUNTING THE OMER ͳ

"Today is Day 16, which is 2 Weeks and 2 Days of the Omer."

The arrogant have viciously ridiculed me, yet I did not turn away from Your Torah. I remember Your judgments from of old, Adonai, and comfort myself. Burning indignation grips me, because of the wicked who forsake Your Torah. Your decrees have become my songs in the house where dwell. (51-54)

My pregnant goat named Grace is dealing with terrible inflammation in her legs due to the stress on her body. She can't walk without great pain, so she kneels on her front legs, sometimes walking on her knees, making her vulnerable to predators. This, of course, increases her anxiety. It will be only Adonai's grace if she lives to see the fruit of her labor. She gets herbal anti-inflammatories, arnica rubs, and I sing to her. Why am I singing? Because studies show that music is helpful in healing inflammation brought on by the release of the stress hormone, cortisol, into our system. Stress causes inflammation.

The inflammatory rhetoric of our culture causes stress, which releases cortisol, which increases inflammation.

In verse 53 of Psalm 119, David confesses inflammatory thoughts toward the wicked who have forsaken Torah. This implies that they once embraced Torah, but now reject Adonai. This is apostasy — a people or nation who once embraced Biblical values, now rejects them.

Like David, our hearts burn for the man who preached Your Word and then renounced You. Or for the person who knew You, who now embraces orthodox Judaism and

Yeshua becomes the great casualty. It would be easy to point a finger at them and forget about the adage that says, "But for the grace of GOD, there go I."

What is David's response when his spirit becomes vexed by the apostates? We already know that David is a music therapist, formerly hired by Saul to soothe his anxiety by driving out the evil spirits that vexed him. So it comes as no surprise that his prescription in the very next verse is to sing songs about Adonai's righteousness. The word for decrees is *chok*/חק and another way to translate it is a "prescribed task." The exact translation of verse 54 is *"Songs have been to me thy statutes (prescribed tasks) in the house of my pilgrimage."*

Adonal, in Your grace may we kneel to Your prescribed task of songs in the night, songs in our pain, and songs through these birth-pangs, until the Kingdom is delivered. Amen!

DECLARE THESE WORDS TODAY: *PRESCRIBED TASKS! 34 Days Left! Shavuot! Pentecost!*

Notes / Prayers / Reflections / Revelations

17 – COUNTING THE OMER ד

"Today is Day 17, which is 2 Weeks and 3 Days of the Omer."

In the night I remember Your Name, Adonai, and keep watching over Your Torah. This is my own: that I keep Your precepts (55-56).

In Day 16, we talked a bit about inflammation. As we continue with that theme, there is something else that is a root cause of inflammation. It's indirectly mentioned there in v. 55. Yes, it is poor sleep. On the run from his pursuers, David probably spent many sleepless nights. What, then, is David's prescription for his insomnia?

Here it is: At night he remembers HaShem. Rather than losing sleep over former believers and their antics, he "self-medicates" with Torah.

What's so beautiful is that he remembers His "Name." Solomon says that *"The name of the LORD is a strong tower; the righteous man runs into it and is safe"* (Proverbs 18:10). David runs to the safety of His Name during the hours of darkness. Adonai is the circumlocution used in place of the unpronounceable name YHVH!

David says He remembers It. I wonder if there was a flashback to the Valley of Elah when he stood face-to-face with the giant Goliath while King Saul's shivering soldiers crouched behind their shields and barricades. Did those memories excite Him to remember, just like it was yesterday, his taunt to the giant? *"You come against me with sword and spear and javelin,"* David said, *"but I come against you in the Name of the LORD Almighty, the God of the armies of Israel, whom you have defied"* (1 Samuel 17:45).

The Name of G-D was his weapon.

Maybe it crossed his mind that the majesty of King Saul paled in comparison to the majestic kingliness of His G-D, so he penned these words in Psalm 8:1: *"O, Lord, our Lord, how majestic is Your Name in all the earth!"* There was no one who could compare to Him, so David makes a declaration about the awesomeness of that Name.

Verse 56 is a puzzle. *"This is my own,"* the Psalmist says. His own what? A precept regulates behavior and thought. So perhaps he's saying that his own regulation for anxiety is to keep his thoughts on Adonai. Look at the verses! When He remembers the Name, He grabs Torah, and he keeps in his heart what he has read about the Name of the LORD Almighty, the GOD of the armies of Israel, about the majesty of the One whom the angels enthrone and all creation worships!

There is your indomitable weapon, my friend. Use it and use it reverently.

DECLARE THESE WORDS TODAY: *His GREAT NAME! Praise Him! Shavuot/Pentecost! 32 Days Left!*

Notes / Prayers / Reflections / Revelations

18 – COUNTING THE OMER ח

"Today is Day 18, which is 2 Weeks and 4 Days of the Omer."

Adonai is my portion. I promised to guard Your words. I have entreated you favor with all my heart. Be gracious to me according to Your word (57-58).

David continues his heart cry to GOD with the bold statement, *"ADONAI is my portion."* The Hebrew word for "portion" is the word *chelek*/חלק (*Strong's* #h2505). In its proper form, it refers to "smoothness." It can also carry the connotation of "an allotment, flattery, inheritance, or portion." It is used for the dividing up of the land in Deuteronomy, and it can refer to inheritance from families and tribes. In Exodus, the Lord tells the Levites that when they get into *Eretz Yisrael* (The Promised Land), they would not be given any land allotment. He tells them that He would be their *chelek*/חלק. In Lamentations 3:24, the concept is carried through again as the writer declares, *"The Lord is my portion,"* says my soul; *"therefore, I will hope in Him."*

Linked to hope is faith. Hebrews 1:1 says that *"Faith is the substance of things hoped for"* and James 2:14 tells us that *"Faith without work is dead."* Our souls can easily be swayed by many things, but it will never be satisfied until it rests in the very place it was designed for. That is why David continues His thought with a promise to guard the word of the LORD. That word "guard" carries the idea of putting a fence around something so that thieves and robbers cannot come in to steal what has been planted and what needs protection. In this passage, it is the Word that needs guarding. He makes a plea of full surrender and desperation. When he does this, he opens the door for G-D to move in his life. Now the favor will come... and so will His grace. You will hasten after what you see as your inheritance ... and David's inheritance was G-D!

David knew that the portion He found in the LORD was a gift freely given, but he also knew that with that gift came responsibility to guard, grow, and to immediately obey.

So what territory are you claiming?

What or who is your portion?

Do you treasure it?

Are you guarding it?

Are you quick to obey or do you delay with a heart that is divided?

When we have David's heart, we can cry out for favor and grace according to His Word, and He will be quick to answer!

DECLARE THESE WORDS TODAY: *My Portion! My Allotment! Shavuot! Counting UP!*

Notes / Prayers / Reflections / Revelations

_____

_____

_____

_____

_____

_____

_____

19 – COUNTING THE OMER ח

"Today is Day 19, which is 2 Weeks and 5 Days of the Omer."

I have considered my ways and turned my feet back to Your testimonies. I hasten and do not delay to obey Your mitzvot. The ropes of the wicked are coiled around me, but I did not forget Your Torah. At midnight I rise to praise You, because of Your righteous rulings. I am a companion of all who fear You, of those who observe Your precepts. The earth is full of Your lovingkindness Adonai—teach me Your decrees (59-64).

In verses 57-58, David recognized where his portion is found. In the verses above, David addresses the struggles the world will place upon those who desire to make the LORD their portion. The Hebrew word for "ropes" is the Hebrew word *chevel*/חבל, and it, too, can be used regarding portioning or allotment.

It is my opinion that David was intentionally juxtaposing the portion that comes from man to the portion that comes from the LORD. One brings freedom; the other brings bondage, if we let it. Proverbs 29:25 states, *"Fear of Man will prove to be a snare, but one who trusts in ADONAI will be kept safe."*

David provides three answers when the ropes of man try to ensnare us, and they are as follows: #1) turning right back to the Truth, and that Truth is found in G-D's word, #2) giving praise in the middle of the trial, and #3) surrounding yourself with those who will build you up in the faith. One can choose to keep company with those who will corrupt. or one can choose to keep company with those who will build up. The same is true with the use of *chevel*/חבל. While the *chevel*/חבל of man will lead to entrapment, the *chevel*/חבל of GOD can lead to abundance. In Psalm 16:5-6, the writer says, *"ADONAI is my portion and my cup. You cast my lot. My boundary lines fall in pleasant places— surely my heritage is beautiful."* There are times that we will feel like David did, ensnared by the troubles of this world, the deeds of wicked men, and the words of hurtful people, but it is in that very moment that we must turn to the Truth of GOD's word and believe, despite what we see. We must agree that what He has said is indeed trustworthy and true. He has given you a beautiful inheritance and it is found in Him.

Claim it. Cling to it. Walk in that Promise. Live out the Victory He has already placed in your hands You have a beautiful Portion!!!

DECLARE THESE WORDS TODAY: *G-D'S CHEVEL! Pleasant Places! Counting UP!*

Notes / Prayers / Reflections / Revelations

20 – COUNTING THE OMER כ

"Today is Day 20, which is 2 Weeks and 6 Days of the Omer."

You do good to Your servant, Adonal, according to Your word. Teach me good sense and knowiedge, for I trusted in Your mitzvot. Before i was afflicted I went astray, but now I keep Your word. You are good and keep doing good- teach me Your decrees (65-68).

In this passage, David continues to use the word "good" over and over to describe G-D and the works that He has done. The Hebrew word for "good" is the word *tov*/(טוב), and it can be used in a variety of contexts. It has to do with maturity, the right timing, and the right place. It can describe people, things, or circumstances, but no matter what, its origin comes back to the One who first spoke the word—Elohim. On each day of creation, He looked at all that He had made, and *"Elohim saw that it was good"* וַיַּרְא אֱלֹהִים כִּי־טוֹב: (Genesis 1:10); moreover, after the creation of man, He saw that His creation was "behold *very* good (*tov meod*)" וְהִנֵּה־טוֹב מְאֹד.

That is why we must proclaim His goodness every day and in every circumstance. May our anthem be like the chorus of a very passionate contemporary worship song: "All my life You have been faithful. All my life you have been so, so good. With every breath that I am able, I will sing of the goodness of G-D."

Furthermore, *tov*/(טוב) is something we obtain, through a humble spirit, that is. A spirit that is willing to learn what G-D desires to teach us. When we recognize He is good, we can be taught lessons that will not just fill our heads, but also transform our lives and make us more like Him.

One school of thought attributes the ancient pictograph of the letter *tet*/(ט) which begins the word *tov*/(טוב) to be a symbol of a basket. A basket is something that holds things within it or surrounds other objects. In this section of the psalm, David elaborates on how He is constantly surrounded by G-D's word and His goodness. It is also a reminder for us to gather up all that the Lord teaches us, remembering that His desire toward us is for good/*tov*/טוב and not for evil.

It's time to remember that G-D wants to do what He promised He would do for His people in Jeremiah 29:10: *"I will visit you, and fulfill My good word toward you..."*

DECLARE THESE WORDS TODAY: *He Is GOOD! #Tov Meod! GOOD Word! Shavuot!*

Notes / Prayers / Reflections / Revelations

21 – COUNTING THE OMER כ

"Today is Day 21, which is 3 Weeks and 0 Days of the Omer."

Though the proud smeared a lie on me, with all my heart I keep Your precepts. Their minds are insensible, but Your Torah is my delight. It is good for me that I was afflicted, so that I may learn Your decrees. The Torah from Your mouth is better to me than thousands of gold and silver pieces (65-68).

    David continues to contrast the lies of the wicked to the Truth that G-D gives. He knows that the lies of man hold no power when compared to the Truth of G-D. He knows that the true treasure is found in the depth and richness of G-D's everlasting Word. It is in this realization that David can speak with confidence regarding the afflictions he has faced and will face. For David the affliction he received was a training ground to walk out the precepts of ADONAI.

    Every affliction, be it spiritual, physical or emotional, has worth and value when we allow them to illuminate the character and nature of G-D. Like David, do we accept the discipline of the Lord?

    Hebrews 12:5-6 exhorts through the words of Proverbs 3:11-12 saying, *"My son, do not take lightly the discipline of ADONAI or lose heart when you are corrected by Him, because ADONAI disciplines the one He loves and punishes every son He accepts."* What is your perspective when you must endure trials?

    James 1:2-3 encourages those who are feeling downcast, outcast, and burdened to *"consider it all joy ... when you encounter various trials, knowing that the testing of your faith produces endurance."* Peter also takes a similar stance in 1 Peter 1:6-7 edifying the reader by saying, *"You rejoice in this greatly, even though now for a little while, if necessary, you have been distressed by various trials. These trials are so that the true metal of your faith (far more valuable than gold, which perishes though refined by fire) may come to light in praise and glory and honor at the revelation of Messiah Yeshua.*

So let us find that true gold in G-D's Word and allow Him to leverage the inevitable and constant trials in our lives to bring forth the pure gold through us.

DECLARE THESE WORDS TODAY: *Acknowledging Him! Pure Gold! Shavuot! Day 21!*

Notes / Prayers / Reflections / Revelations

22 – COUNTING THE OMER י

"Today is Day 22, which is 3 Weeks and 1 Day of the Omer."

Your hands have made me and formed me. Give me understanding that I may learn Your mitzvot. Those in awe of You see me and rejoice, because I put my hope in Your word (73-74).

This section begins with the letter "yod" (י) and is introduced by the word *"yadecha"*/ ידיך which means "your hands"; therefore, hand begins with the letter "yod" (י).

"Yod" (י) is the smallest letter in the Hebrew alphabet, and it means in the Paleo Hebrew: "work, a deed, to make." The mighty hand that David speaks of, of course, is the hand of G-D, and that single hand has been instrumental in birthing a nation, bringing it forth out of captivity, and establishing it in its Land.

Consider the proclamations of the works and deeds of His Hand (*yadav*/ יָדָיו) in other scriptures:
• Psalm 95:5 says, *"His hands formed the dry land";*
• in Isaiah 48:13, it is GOD Himself who says that His hand (*yadav*/ יָדָיו) founded the earth;
• in Isaiah 64:8, Isaiah declares, *"we are the work of Your hand (yadecha/ ידיך)";*
• Psalm 95:4 says, *"in his hands (yadav/ יָדָיו) are the depths of the earth";*
• Job 12:10 affirms that *"in His hand (yadav/ יָדָיו) is the life of every living thing";*
• Psalm 31:15 says, *"My times are in Your hand (yadecha/ ידיך)";*

- Isaiah 40:12 asks the question: *"Who has measured the waters in the hollow of his hand (yadav/ יָדָיו); and marked off the heavens by the span."*
- Psalm 145:16 says, *"You open Your hand (yadecha/ ידיך) and satisfy the desire of every living thing."*
- In 1 Chronicles 29:12 King David proclaims to Adonai during the commissioning of his son Solomon, *"... in your hand (yadecha/ ידיך) is power and might."*

David reflects the truth of his own existence in our Scriptural context: *"Your hands (yadecha/ ידיך) made me and formed me..."*; therefore, *"give me understanding."* Why does he want understanding? So that he can learn the *mitzvot*. When he learns them, he can learn more about this amazing G-D and His mighty hand... the finger of which etched the heavens (Psalm 8:3), wrote the 10 words on tablets of stone (Ex 31:18), carved His Torah on the fleshy tables of the heart (Jer. 31:33), and that same finger wrote a woman's freedom in the dirt! (John 8:8)

Y*adav*/יָדָיו! His works! His deeds! His hand!

In His hand (*yadav*/יָדָיו) is Power and might! Remember this truth on the 22nd Day of Counting the Omer as you, too, cry for greater understanding, learn His mitzvot, be seen by others and thus others will see Him in you.

DECLARE THESE WORDS TODAY: His Hand! His Finger! His Works! His Deeds! Shavuot! Pentecost!

Notes / Prayers / Reflections / Revelations

_____

_____

_____

_____

23 – COUNTING THE OMER י

"Today is Day 23, which is 3 Weeks and 2 Days of the Omer."

I know, Adonai, Your judgments are just. In faithfulness You have afflicted me. May Your lovingkindness comfort me, according to Your promise to Your servant (75-76).

The 75th verse also begins with the letter *yod* (י), introduced by the word *yadati*/ידעתי, which means, "I know." What is it that the psalmist knows? He knows that the judgments of G-D are righteous! What does that mean? It means every one of G-D's acts is meant to bring forth His purpose and is not connected to our whims! As David said, *"He has not treated us according to our sins, or repaid us according to our iniquities"* (Psalm 103:20). "G-D is out to get me!" you say. "NO," I say, "He's out to bring forth His plans! Those plans are the ones that are good for you!"

David says that when he is afflicted, it is out of G-D's faithfulness, righteousness and His justice! I've got some questions for David:

Do you mean when you ran from King Saul who wanted to kill you, and from your son Absalom who usurped your throne, and when your innocent baby died as a result of your sin with Bathsheba, and what about your servant Uzziah? He was struck dead, simply because he wanted to keep the Ark from falling. What about in your own house; your daughter is abused by her half-brother? (2 Samuel 13). In all of that, GOD is faithful, David? In all of that, He is just?

And David would answer with a resounding, reverberating, "Yes!" This is not just a head knowledge that David has. It is an experiential knowing ... that's the essence of the word "YADAH" in *yadati* / ידעתי! It means that David walked through each of the above moments and every event in his life WITH G-D, trusting Him, loving Him and knowing that even though his own actions brought a lot of these events upon himself, that G-D was faithful and just, even in the consequences of David's actions. No external factor could ever change that!

Therefore, he calls upon the Lord's loving kindness to comfort him because that's what G-D promised. He promised us comfort to the point that He would send His Comforter, the *Ruach HaKodesh*, to us, who would lead, guide, and direct us into all truths.

On this 23rd day of Counting the Omer, look back over your life and see what you were brought from and what you were brought through, and in retrospect to see that maybe your actions brought some of these events upon yourself, and all the while seeing in the midst of them that G-D IS FAITHFUL AND ALL HIS JUDGMENTS ARE JUST!

Remember, He promised to comfort you as you walk with Him, as you get to know (ידי/*yadah*) Him!

Let *yadati* / ידעתי/ "I know," which begins with the smallest letter in the Hebrew alphabet, be your BIGGEST declaration today: **I KNOW** *yadati* / ידעתי, ABBA, that all of Your judgments are just.

DECLARE THESE WORDS TODAY: YADAH! I KNOW! CountingUp! Shavuot!

Notes / Prayers / Reflections / Revelations

_____

_____

24 – COUNTING THE OMER ׳

"Today is Day 24, which is 3 Weeks and 3 Days of the Omer."

May the proud be put to shame for wronging me with a lie, but I will meditate on Your precepts. Let those in awe of You return to me- those who know Your testimonies. My heart will have integrity in following Your decrees, so that I would not be ashamed (78-80).

"To whom much is given much is required" (Luke 12:48). And David was given much, actually he was given much responsibility, much recognition to the point that he becomes the King of all Israel, called a man after G-D's own heart, the very progenitor of King Messiah. So it is not unusual that many lies and accusations would be hurled against David. Knowing what a sensitive man he was to the things of G-D, we can see why he was so affected by these words of slander, especially when all you want to do is good, but your good is abused!

So he prayed that those who slandered him would be put to shame; however, he resolved that in spite of those lies he would not be moved from meditating on the precepts of the Word of G-D. He knew that there were many who stood in awe of G-D; those are the ones he wanted to return to him. David knew that it would take many to give G-D just a fraction of the praise and exaltation that He deserved. So he knew that there were those among his people who knew the testimony of Torah. And he also knew that despite anything else, what was more important was the integrity that he had in following all of G-D's decrees.

I know a young woman who only wanted G-D; everything she did, she wanted to do for Him. People misconstrued her talents and gifts, her determination and drive! She was labeled a charlatan by most of those she had served. She repented where there may have been fault, AND she rested in the truth of G-D's words! He knew her heart! She followed His decrees! And though the situation was intended to bring her shame, she refused to be ashamed because she trusted G-D!

Friends, trust in the Word of G-D! You may be attacked with lies, slander and by those who are proud! You may ask, as David did, that they be put to "shame" / *yash'voo* / ישבו, and though you may never see them put to shame ... anchor yourself in His precepts and statutes ... so that YOU will not be ashamed.

DECLARE THESE WORDS TODAY: *No Shame! Counting Up! Shavuot! Pentecost!*

Notes / Prayers / Reflections / Revelations

25 – COUNTING THE OMER ב

"Today is Day 25, which is 3 Weeks and 4 Days of the Omer."

My soul faints with longing for Your salvation, but I still hope in Your word. My eyes are worn out longing for Your promise, saying, 'When will You comfort me?' Though I became like a wineskin dried in smoke, I do not forget Your decrees (81-83).

"*A wineskin dried in smoke*" gives the sense of being shriveled and dehydrated by the process of smoking. This is what Psalmist compares himself to as he waits upon the salvation and unfulfilled promises of the Lord.

Waiting is very difficult. I remember trying to give our pre-adolescent son lessons on waiting. When he selected the restaurant where we would eat out, it was always a buffet. When it was my turn to select, I always took him to a restaurant where he had to wait for his meal. And he would always say, "Why are they called waiters when we are the ones who are waiting?"

It is in those moments of waiting that we can become, like the Psalmist, seemingly shriveled from the heat and dehydrated from the smoke of waiting... our *souls fainting kal'tah / כָּלְתָה with the longing for salvation.*

But the Psalmist knew that even in those times of waiting it was a necessity that he would hold on to the statutes of GOD. In those times there are many moments where we will cry to the Lord for salvation, and it will appear that salvation is not on the horizon.

There will be times when we will be so excited about the promises of GOD, but we will grow weary in our waiting.

There was nothing like having a prophet visit my former church when I was a younger believer. We waited in line for that prophetic word, or we waited for him to call us forth, to speak into our lives "what thus saith at the Lord."

And then, there would be the waiting game. Is this going to come true? How long must I wait before I stop believing? There were prophetic promises of husbands, wives, vacations, financial increase, houses, land, spiritual heights and promotions. And some of us waited, and waited for the fulfillment of the prophecies, until we became like those wineskins hanging in the smokehouse. What HaShem has given us to stand on is not a prophetic voice (though I'm not discounting the prophetic), but He has given us *"a more sure word of prophecy"* (2 Peter 1:19). It is the voice emanating from the written Word of GOD that says, *"Hope thou in GOD, for I shall yet trust **him** who is the health of my countenance and **my** GOD"* (bold mine) (Psalm 42:11).

And so we wait... But we wait in hope .. shriveled sometimes... but holding on to His decrees!

DECLARE THESE WORDS TODAY: *Shriveled But Hoping! Counting Up! Waiting! Shavuot! 24 More Days!*

Notes / Prayers / Reflections / Revelations

_____

_____

_____

_____

_____

_____

_____

26 – COUNTING THE OMER ב

"Today is Day 26, which is 3 Weeks and 5 Days of the Omer."

How many are the days of Your servant? When will You execute judgment on my persecutors? The proud have dug pits for me—that is not in accord with Your Torah! All Your mitzvot are faithful. They persecute me with a lie—help me! They almost finished me off on earth. But I—I will not forsake Your precepts. Revive me with Your lovingkindness, so I may keep Your mouth's testimony (84-88).

    You know, I have found that, sometimes, people can be quite pretentious - wanting people to believe that their faith is strong when it is not. How many times have you given a false sense of "fine" to those who asked how you were doing? How many times have you worn your mask? Maybe you were raised to believe that you should never allow anyone to see you hurting or to see that your world is not as stable as you let on. Well, I am so glad that the psalmist is not one of those people. I so appreciate the fact that he is "real." It reminds me of a poem by Langston Hughes, "Mother to Son." The mother persona says to her son,
    Life for me ain't been no crystal stair.
    It's had tacks in it,
    And splinters, And boards torn up,
    And places with no carpet on the floor—
    Bare.
    Take for instance, when the book of Job starts, it is hasatan (the adversary) that has come to El Shaddai (G-D Almighty), and it is He who allows hasatan to afflict Job.

And when Job is afflicted, he does not credit the enemy with his affliction, but he acknowledges the source of his affliction as being El Shaddai. I believe he knew that G-D was sovereign over all things, and that if El Shaddai allowed affliction, even though it felt like it was to his detriment, it was for his good. And I sense that the Psalmist has the same sentiments as Job who says, *"Though he slays me, yet will I trust him"* (Job 13:15). The Psalmist knows that life is difficult, and more difficulties will come (tacks, splinters, and boards torn up), but the hope must be in the statutes of El Shaddai for only in them can he hope.

It is true, life ain't no crystal stair... But there is always the truth of Torah. The mother continues to tell her son:

So boy, don't you turn back.
Don't you set down on the steps
'Cause you finds it's kinder hard.
Don't you fall now—
For I'se still goin', honey,
I'se still climbin'.

You keep climbing, too, because there is Torah - there is no fault in it! Like the Psalmist, know that the lies and persecution of the enemy are meant to harm you, but the *mitzvot* from G-D are for your edification ... because like the mother to her son, you will find that *"life ain't no crystal stair."* Just keep climbing!

DECLARE THESE WORDS TODAY: *Not Giving Up! Torah Is My Goal! Shavuot/Pentecost! 23 More Days!*

Notes / Prayers / Reflections / Revelations

_____

_____

_____

_____

27 – COUNTING THE OMER ל

"Today is Day 26, which is 3 Weeks and 5 Days of the Omer."

Forever, Adonai, Your word stands firm in the heavens. Your faithfulness endures from generation to generation. You established the earth, and it stands. Your judgements stand today, for all things are Your servants (89-91).

I see You and Your Torah in everything. My day changes as I either lean into or choose not to lean into Your commandments. You remain the same - not just for me, but for every person who exists, has existed, and is yet to be born. When I read Your word, it is You reading to me - like a father reading to a child. As I hear Your voice, my heart is responding and basking in Your presence. I hear Your heartbeat in every word, and I see the love you have for each person and the tender care You took to make sure that we know Your thoughts and plans for us. I must not let Your word remain a mystery to me!

This Word that some of us allow to be a mystery stands forever! Do you know that there is no word in the English language for the Hebrew word *la'neh'tzach* / לנצח? which we translate as "forever"? Forever is a place where there is no time. Imagine that! No morning or night. No clocks, sundials or watches. What is that like? I have no idea. Even better, there is no space. There is this image in Ezekiel 1 of a phantom, surreal creature with four faces moving in all directions at once ... because there is no direction beyond space and time.

Ezekiel says, *"they did not turn when they moved; each could move in the direction of any of its faces"* (1:9). And David says, it is in that place where the Word of the Lord is firmly settled, established and fixed. As fixed as His Word is ... that's how enduring His faithfulness is. You can't outlive it, outrun it, outlast it. David says this in Psalm 139:7-8, *"Where can I go to escape Your Spirit? Where can I flee from Your presence? If I ascend to the heavens, You are there; if I make my bed in Sheol, You are there."*

There is nowhere we can go beyond His presence or outside His watchful eye. In one of Yeshua's teachings, He assures His audience that they have a Heavenly Father who sees everything: *"What is the price of two sparrows—one copper coin? But not a single sparrow can fall to the ground without your Father knowing it"* (Matthew 10:29). When we have this kind of access to the Father and His Word, GOD forbid that it remains a mystery!

DECLARE THESE WORDS TODAY: *Forever Settled! Counting Up! Shavuot/Pentecost! 22 More Days!*

Notes / Prayers / Reflections / Revelations

_____

_____

_____

_____

_____

_____

_____

28 – COUNTING THE OMER ל

"Today is Day 28, which is 4 Weeks and 0 Days of the Omer."

If Your Torah had not been my delight, I would have perished in my affliction. I will never forget Your precepts. For with them You have kept me alive. I am Yours, save me! For I have sought out Your precepts. The wicked wait for me to destroy me. But I will study your testimonies. I have seen a limit to all perfection, yet your commandment is boundless (92-96).

How can I lay down Your voice, Your everlasting word that is your Torah? It calls to me upon waking and nudges me earnestly in my sleep. It seeks to pierce through anxiety and fear so that the voice, Your Voice, will cause me to breathe and then breathe again. Who am I? Who am I?! that You are so intent on moving alongside me, close and present. You see the plans of the enemy and harm that is spoken; but, You have stationed me in strength and I am able to move boldly in Your authority. Your word opens doors I never knew existed. The beauty and life of Your word surround me every second of my day. I will stand in Your presence and learn to love as You have loved me.

I hope this can become your daily meditation as I want it to be for me. If desiring GOD this much is what caused GOD to call David, *"a man after his own heart,"* then we have the instructions on being called such a man or woman.

The Psalmist says, *"If Your Torah had not been my delight ..."* The Hebrew word for "delight" is actually a plural intensive noun. "Delights"/*Sha'a shoo eem*/שַׁעֲשׁוּעִים!

Are you getting this? Are you dealing with an affliction that compromises your faith, that causes you to charge G-D foolishly? The death of a spouse. The death of a child? A chronic illness or pain? Bankruptcy! Infidelity in a relationship? Every one of these situations is difficult. Affliction has a way of causing people to turn from G-D by asking the age-old question: "How could He have allowed this to happen?"

The Psalmist says that there was no way he could overcome the affliction in his life if Torah had not been his "delights"/*sha'a shoo eem*/שַׁעֲשׁוּעִים! Don't you want that for your life? Make Torah your delights!

He even goes so far as to say Torah has kept him alive. There are limitations he has seen in the earth, but there is no limitation with G-D's Word!

Oh, that Torah could be our "delights"/*sha'a shoo eem*/שַׁעֲשׁוּעִים! Oh, that we could wrap ourselves in the boundless nature of His Word. We can ... let's study His testimonies ... together.

DECLARE THESE WORDS TODAY: *Torah-My-Delights! Counting Up! Shavuot/Pentecost! 21MoreDays!*

Notes / Prayers / Reflections / Revelations

_____

_____

_____

_____

_____

_____

29 – COUNTING THE OMER מ

"Today is Day 29, which is 4 Weeks and 1 Day of the Omer."

Oh how I love your Torah. It is my meditation all day, Your mitzvot make me wiser than my enemies - for they are mine forever. I have more insight than all my teachers, for your testimonies are my meditations. I have gained more understanding than all my elders, for I have kept your precepts (97-100).

The letter *mem* (מ) symbolizes water, mighty massive, chaos (like the deep) to come from (like water down a stream). The letter *mem* (מ) itself, however, literally means "from." King David is virtually shouting, "Your Torah is 'from' where LIFE, WISDOM, and INSIGHT come!" Just as we must have water to survive, water also has another quality of filling every area, crevasse and crack available to it…it will not leave any surface parched that has been freely exposed to it. The Torah is the Word of LIFE, Living Water *"Mayim Chayim"*! How blessed are we to have Living Water from the Torah that we can pick up, study, memorize, and live from!

King David points out that though teachers and elders are valuable, that personally, from the Torah, application of the commandments gives him personal wisdom above his enemies; it gives him meditations on which to keep his mind fixed, and it gives him understanding! Oh, how we desire and benefit from these in our lives as well!

In Colossians 3:2-4 Paul encouraged, *"Focus your mind on things above, not on things on the earth. For you have died, and your life is hidden with Messiah in GOD. When*

Messiah, who is your life, is revealed, then you also will be revealed with Him, in glory!" Selah! The following verses support values brought forth in the Torah; they are inseparably linked together as James 2:26 says, *"For just as the body without the spirit is dead, so also faith without works is dead."* HaShem wants us to LIVE, to be alive and active in Him.

It is beyond valuable to learn from our teachers and elders as they bring forth the Torah and cast the vision for us as a Body, uniting us in worship and truth. King David, though, is emphasizing that our personal, intimate habits in the way we walk out our lives daily is so enriched by the Word: it is to be our focus. It is how we can receive valuable wisdom-and-insight-filled-communique from the *Ruach HaKodesh* just for our ears and edification.

What a personal GOD King David served, and He is the same yesterday, today forever!! So we "get" to serve Him, too! *HalleluŸah*!!

DECLARE THESE WORDS TODAY: *Mayim Chayim! Counting Up! 20 More Days! Shavuot!*

Notes / Prayers / Reflections / Revelations

_____

_____

_____

_____

_____

_____

_____

30 – COUNTING THE OMER מ

"Today is Day 30, which is 4 Weeks and 2 Days of the Omer."

I kept my feet from every evil way, in order to follow Your word. I do not turn away from your rulings, for you Yourself have taught me. How sweet is your word to my taste — yes, sweeter than honey to my mouth! From your precepts I get discernment, therefore I hate every false way (101-104).

As we discovered yesterday in the first section of *mem* (מ), that the word "from" is pivotal. The point being, **where/who** is our source? To follow HaShem's Word, we are to: 1) keep from every evil way in order to follow Torah; 2) not turn from His rulings which HaShem personally teaches; and 3) not to turn from His precepts so that we have discernment, learn to hate evil, and can then make the choice to cling to what is good. The rotation of these three is cyclical. The Scriptures are laid out in a self-revolving manner to reinforce these principles. King David clearly defines from what position he gleans LIFE.

There is a lovely tradition in Judaism when a child is learning their letters in the process of learning to read Torah. The teacher will use a board with the Hebrew letters written on it and put honey on the letters. They then instruct the child to lick off the honey and say, "Darling, lick!" How clever! This is so precious and King David says the Torah is even sweeter!

Being on Day 30, we're anticipating the arrival of Shavuot to celebrate the giving of the *Ruach HaKodesh* and the Torah! We're 19 days away!!! Let's have that same excitement that the 120 in the Upper Room had. How amazing that we can personally connect with the Creator of Heaven and Earth and thus be more personally ready to corporately enter into His presence when we meet together; He promised to be there when even two or three are gathered in His Name!!

Psalms 34:8-11 says, *"The Angel of Adonai encamps around those who fear Him, and delivers them. Taste and see how good Adonai is. Blessed is the one who takes refuge in Him. Fear Adonai, his kedoshim, For those who fear Him lack nothing."* Just as the Psalmist anticipated eating of the sweetness of Torah, let's be that excited about the portal that will be opened between Heaven and earth in 19 Days! Enjoy your 30th Day!

DECLARE THESE WORDS TODAY: *Darling Lick! Counting Up! Pentecost/Shavuot Awaits! Day30!*

Notes / Prayers / Reflections / Revelations

_____

_____

_____

_____

_____

_____

_____

_____

31 – COUNTING THE OMER ב

"Today is Day 31, which is 4 Weeks and 3 Days of the Omer."

Thy word is a lamp unto my feet, and a light unto my path. I have sworn, and I will perform it, that I will keep thy righteous judgments. I am afflicted very much: quicken me, O Lord, according unto thy word. Accept, I beseech thee, the freewill offerings of my mouth, O Lord, and teach me thy judgments (105-108).

This section of Psalm 119 is introduced by the letter *nun* (נ). There is an interpretation of the Hebrew alphabet from the Sages that implies that the bent *nun* (נ) and the straight *nun* (ן) refer to a faithful person who is bent (נ), completely devoted to GOD, subservient to His will, but will ultimately become a well-known faithful person *nun* (ן) (*Shabbos* 104a 4-5). SO, as we peer into the words of the Psalmist in this section, let us bend ourselves in reverence by committing our ways devotedly to GOD.

Proclaim this within the depths of your inner being: "Yeshua, the Word of GOD, is a lamp to my feet." Yeshua is not just *the* lamp to our path, but He is the very Source of Light that lives within our souls.

Proverbs 6:23 states that *"The commandments are a lamp and the Torah is a light; reproofs of instruction are the way of life."* When I think about a lamp, I'm reminded that it goes dim. But the Word does not go dim, NO WAY! Because I turned away from the lamp, it appears dim, or because I didn't have enough oil for my lamp; maybe the wear and tear of life's path caused my lamp to go dim, or more specifically, I did not humble myself to the Word. No matter what is the cause of your dim lamp, there is a greater Source of light— Yeshua the Light of the world.

Yeshua is not just a lamp that we hold that may need more batteries, more oil, a new wick.

Yeshua is THE Light/*ohr*/אור) to our path, the very Source of our light, a continuous Source of light. But we must turn ourselves to the Light by abiding in Him. *"If you abide in me, my Word will abide in you…"* (John 15:5-7), Yeshua says. We must abide *actively*. Abiding is more than a passive being in His presence. We must abide by committing and settling in and building an abode in the commandments, statutes, and the Torah, which lead us to Yeshua (John 15:10). We keep the commandments by doing actions of love or *mitzvot*. These are the actions that we must do to continuously turn ourselves toward Yeshua, the Light to our Path.

DECLARE THESE WORDS TODAY: *Abiding! The Bent-and-Straight Nun! Pentecost/Shavuot! 22 Days!*

Notes / Prayers / Reflections / Revelations

_____

_____

_____

_____

_____

_____

_____

32 – COUNTING THE OMER ב

"Today is Day 32, which is 4 Weeks and 3 Days of the Omer."

My soul is continually in danger, yet I have not forgotten Your Torah. The wicked have set a snare for me, yet I did not stray from Your precepts. Your testimonies I have as a heritage forever, for they are my heart's joy. I turned my heart to do Your decrees, forever, to the very end (109-112).

Remember that thought you were holding from our previous devotional? "We are made perfect or complete through unison with Yeshua." This word perfect is "shalom" and relates in various ways with *nesh'va'ti*/ נִשְׁבַּעְתִּי. (Psalm 119:106); the root word שָׁבַע means "to seven or complete oneself by affirmation." Our paths are perfected or affirmed when we are made perfect through Yeshua, the Light of our path. We are reminded many times in the Word to be perfect.

Yeshua himself states *"Therefore, you shall be perfect, just as your Father in heaven is perfect"* (Matthew 5:48). As we have studied in the past, perfection is not determined by how we walk the path, which would be the quality of our walk ... but *with whom* we walk the path, which refers to the quality of our relationship. Perfection is a covenant relationship that Yeshua fulfills. And because of our covenant relationship, we have a great inheritance. Our inheritance (the commands and statutes of the Torah), which serve as testimonies of GOD, are all that we need to live a life of godliness and walk in the path of light. In today's verses, we will see that despite various oppositions, as we incline our heart to pursue and obey GOD by taking hold of our inheritance with all our heart, soul, might, and mind, it will keep us on the path where Yeshua lights the way. We will never stay in darkness because the darkness can never extinguish the light (John 1:5).

In verse 109, we see that our own free will, or the lot we choose for our souls, can draw us away from the light. And as the sages put it, the danger we bring ourselves into can dim our light. The Psalmist says, *"I constantly take my life in my hands, yet I do not forget Your Torah."*

So, again as we peer into today's verses, let's actively bend ourselves like the letter *nun* (נ), bowing in reverence to G-D wholeheartedly, taking firm hold of Yeshua. Let's do something different today. When you see the *nun* (נ), bow like we do when we say "Blessed" in the liturgical prayers as an action of committing yourself to G-D's Word.

DECLARE THESE WORDS TODAY: *Seven Yourself! Nun (נ)! A Great Inheritance! Shavuot!*

Notes / Prayers / Reflections / Revelations

33 – COUNTING THE OMER ס

"Today is Day 33, which is 4 Weeks and 5 Days of the Omer."

I hate double-minded ones, but Your Torah I love. You are my hiding place and my shield - in Your word I hope. Away from me, evildoers, so I may keep the mitzvot of my God! Sustain me according to Your word, so I may live, and let me not be ashamed of my hope. Support me and I will be saved, and study Your decrees continually (113-117). (Lag B'Omer*)

The letter that introduces this portion of Psalm 119 is the *samech* (*sa'me'ach*) (ס), which is pronounced as an "s"; the word *"samech"* means "secret." The word that begins this portion is *say'a'fim* / סֵעֲפִים which means "ambivalent thoughts." The TLV translates it as "double-minded."

I get what David is saying. I'm sure you understand, too. One of the worst things for Yeshua was hypocrisy, and that is, in essence, "double mindedness." He says, (Mt. 6:24). James goes on to say, *"A double-minded man is unstable in all of his ways"* (James 1:8). Yeshua tells his talmidim in Matthew 16:6, *"Beware the leaven of the Pharisees,"* and that leaven is hypocrisy; that's when you say one thing and do another; when you do not practice what you preach.

When Torah becomes your looking glass and everything is perceived through it, you will hate what G-D hates and you will love what G-D loves. David wanted to be so far away from evil doers, anything that would prevent him from walking in the *mitzvot*.

I heard a Pastor say, "I love preaching; it's the people that give me a hard time." Oh, that we could run away and do Torah only.

Unfortunately, or *rather* fortunately, we *cannot* do Torah apart from "doing" people.

What are we to do — those of us who understand the truth of the Word - and have to deal with hypocrisy, double mindedness, and evildoers on a regular basis? I think David found the *samech* - the secret: that *samech* is in verse 116; WE MUST BE *"sustained"* by the Word. The world may hate Torah, but that does not, and should not, mitigate your keeping of Torah. Some may love you today and hate you tomorrow, but that should not affect the love that you should have for them. How do we get through it all? The evildoers? The ups and downs? Shame? Try the "samech" expressed in verses 116 and 117 again: **Sustain me** *sam'ka'ne* / סָמְכֵנִי... **Support me** *s'ah'da'ne* / סְעָדֵנִי.. according to your Word ... *"and I shall be saved."*

Declare these words today: *Samech! Sustained By the Word! Supported By the Word! Shavuot!*

Notes / Prayers / Reflections / Revelations

_____

_____

_____

_____

_____

_____

_____

34 – COUNTING THE OMER ס

"Today is Day 34, which is 4 Weeks and 6 Days of the Omer."

You despise all who wander from Your decrees, for their deceitfulness is in vain. All the wicked of the earth You remove like dross. Therefore I love Your testimonies. My flesh shudders for fear of You, and I am in awe of Your judgments (118-120).

 Sa'lee'ta / סָלִיתָ is the word that begins verse 118. It means "to regard lightly, to toss aside"; in the TLV it is translated as "despise" and the KJV translates it as "trodden down." The word, of course, begins with a *samech* (ס). In our last entry, we discovered that "samech" means "secret." Its paleo-Hebrew image can also denote a "prop" or "a pillar," something that supports.
 What we see in the three verses cited above are three personas. The first would be one who wanders from the Lord's decrees. According to David, attempting to deceive others by claiming to uphold the Lord's decrees is vanity; it's worthless, nothing, futile. These people have no support, nothing to stand on. Solomon says this about vanity: *"I looked at everything done on earth, and I saw that it is all a waste of time. It is like trying to catch the wind"* (Ecclesiastes 1:14 ERV). Now that's futility!
 The second persona is the "wicked." They simply have no support in this world. They are like dross, which is "the **discarded** scum that forms on the top when a precious metal is being refined." At one point, HaShem says this of Israel when they descend into idolatry: *"...the people of Israel are the worthless slag that remains after silver is*

smelted. They are the dross that is left over—a useless mixture of copper, tin, iron, and lead" (Ezekiel 22:18).

Then there is the third persona - the psalmist. He realizes the difference. Whereas persona #1 does not love the testimonies of HaShem, the psalmist says that he does. He is overcome with a Godly Fear when he realizes the fates of the ones who despise HaShem's decrees and the fate of the wicked. They have nothing to stand on. They are ships without sails. Boats without anchors. Houses built upon sinking sand.

David's *samech* (ס) — his pillar and his support — is what he has been telling us over and over again since the first verse of Psalm 119: it is Torah, the laws, statutes, and testimonies of HaShem.

May they be your (ס) *samech*, as well.

DECLARE THESE WORDS TODAY: *Torah! My Support! MyPillar! Shavuot/Pentecost!*

Notes / Prayers / Reflections / Revelations

35 – COUNTING THE OMER ע

"Today is Day 35, which is 5 Weeks and 0 Days of the Omer."

I did what is just and right. Do not leave me to my oppressors. Guarantee Your servant's well-being. Do not let arrogant ones oppress me. My eyes fail, longing for Your salvation and for Your righteous word. Deal with Your servant as befits Your lovingkindness, and teach me Your statutes (121-124).

David has quite a few requests here for HaShem. If you have been reading the Psalm with us up to this point, you know that his requests are not new. As we consider this, let's take a look at the letter that begins this portion of the psalm: *ayin* (ע); it means "eye." It has a lot to do with the way we see things.

Here's <u>David's perception</u>, which is very much like ours. He starts out with myopic vision ... I have done everything that I know to do to serve You, HaShem! I have treated others justly and fairly the way you desire. When I realize that I have trespassed, I am quick to repent.

<u>This is our myopia</u>: I give my tithes and offerings. I pray, do *mitzvot*, and follow the Golden Rule. So where are You, G-D? Why am I being tormented by my enemies? Why am I being oppressed? Why are you not guaranteeing that I am not harmed?

<u>True perception:</u> The safest place in the whole world is in the will of G-D, but it is not a place free from trouble, pain, hurt or disappointment.

In my childhood church, there was this deacon who never seemed to be involved in wrongdoings... he was the chairman deacon, after all; he was in the choir, and led the congregation in prayer. I'm sure he gave tithes and offerings. When he became ill with lung cancer, my mom and I went to visit him. I remember this as if it were yesterday. He said, "I don't know how I got this. I never smoked cigarettes or drank liquor. I didn't do any of those things! And here I am with cancer." And yes, he died. May his memory be for a blessing!

I am not judging this man, but I was so saddened by the sentiments of a life lived with such dedication to the Lord; now when affliction comes, there is a big question of why? Paul and Barnabas said this to the believers in Lystra when Paul was stoned to death and dragged outside of the city: *"We must go through many hardships to enter the kingdom of God"* (Acts 14:22). Who was more righteous than these two - Paul and Barnabas?

David finds his *ayin* (ע), the right perspective, in verse 24. Let me paraphrase: Whatever befalls me, HaShem, let it be according to Your lovingkindness. If I have to go through whatever ... in the midst of my going through, teach me your statutes.

Beloved, this should be your *ayin* (ע), too.

DECLARE THESE WORDS TODAY: *The Right Vision! Teach Me Your Ways! Counting Up! Pentecost/ Shavuot!*

Notes / Prayers / Reflections / Revelations

_____

_____

_____

_____

36 – COUNTING THE OMER ע

"Today is Day 36, which is 5 Weeks and 1 Days of the Omer."

I am Your servant, give me discernment, so I may understand Your testimonies. It is time for Adonai to act — they have violated Your Torah! Therefore I love Your mitzvot more than gold, more than pure gold. Therefore I esteem all Your precepts as right in every way—every false way I hate (125-128).

I believe that most of the readers of this devotional know that King David was not able to build the Temple for the Lord, although he wanted to. Instead, ADONAI told him that his son Solomon would build the Temple. So what does David do? He begins to prepare all the materials that Solomon would need to build G-D a House! No doubt he remembered saying, *"Here I am, living in a house of cedar, while the ark of the covenant of the LORD is under a tent"* (1 Chronicles 17:1). Even though he was not able to build the Temple, he spared no expense in securing as many of the products needed.

In the above verses, David is again reiterating his love for the Word of G-D by using four of the five words that stand for some aspect of the Word: *"testimonies"* (125) *a'dah* /עֵדָה; *"torah"* (126); תּוֹרָה; *"commandments"* (127); *"mitzvah"* מִצְוָה; *"precepts"*/ *pe'koo'dim* / פִּקּוּדִים. Not only does he esteem G-D's Word to the point that he hates everything that is contrary to it, but he also prays for discernment so that he can understand it. I believe he was aware of the same truth that Peter wrote in his epistle, *"... no prophecy of the scripture is of any private interpretation"* (1:20). Therefore, he wanted discernment so that he would know HaShem's intention behind the words He spoke. Discernment should be a constant prayer of ours as well.

He uses in this section a comparison that only David could really understand. He says, *"Therefore I love Your mitzvot more than pure gold."* One website says, "When [David] prepared for the house of GOD, it took 1,086 talents of gold to build the Temple"; that means "about 34 tons of gold were brought to Jerusalem from Ophir by Solomon's workers. This quantity, worth about $125 million at today's prices, is thought to have constituted about half the known gold supply of the ancient world."

And David had access to all of that - half the known gold supply of the ancient world. It's easy for us to say, "I love the Word more than gold" if we have no gold or just a minimum amount! But he had access to half the world's gold... and all of that gold did not compare to the love he had for G-D's Commandments, His Precepts, Testimonies = His Torah!

Maybe there is something that you have in abundance! Do you love His Word more than that!?

DECLARE THESE WORDS TODAY: *More Than That! Counting Up! Pentecost/Shavuot!*

Notes / Prayers / Reflections / Revelations

_____

_____

_____

_____

_____

37 – COUNTING THE OMER פ

"Today is Day 37, which is 5 Weeks and 2 Days of the Omer."

Your testimonies are wonderful. Therefore my soul obeys them. The unfolding of Your words gives light, giving understanding to the simple (129-131).

The letter *pe* (פ) means "mouth." Even the shape of the פ, according to the Rabbinic sages, gives the appearance of an open mouth to speak and the final *pe* (ף) resembles a closed mouth to be silent (Shabbat 104a).

When you think of an open mouth, what do you think of? I think of a baby bird with its beak wide open waiting in hungry expectation to eat from its mother's provision. Let's meditate upon the word and paint an image of this open mouth, the letter *pe* (פ). The Psalmist says, *"Your testimonies are wonderful"* (פְּלָאוֹת עֵדְוֹתֶיךָ / *p'la'ot ad'o'te'cha*); *"Therefore my soul keeps them."*

This root of *p'la'ot*/ פְּלָאוֹת, which is *peleh* / פֶּלֶא, means "extraordinary, hard to understand, to marvel"! Everything that is a testimony of G-D is WONDERFUL.

"Your testimonies" (*ad'o'te'cha* / עֵדְוֹתֶיךָ) comes from the root word, *ad* / עד meaning "witness." G-D's *testimonies* consist of those things that are a *witness* of His power. And just like the *pe* (פ), when we see the testimonies of G-D, if we love Him with a reverential fear, then our mouths may hang open in awe of His greatness. *Peleh* / פֶּלֶא, is the same root that Jeremiah 32:17 uses to describe the works of G-D. I can imagine that when Jeremiah prayed to G-D, he prayed

with an open mouth in awe of G-D's greatness, proclaiming, *"There is nothing too wonderful for You."* Open your mouth in awe of G-D's greatness! His greatness is beyond our understanding (Psalm 145:3)!

Just as G-D gave the Israelites manna as a testimony of His gratitude provision in the wilderness to be remembered for generations (Exodus 16:32-35), so He gave us Yeshua, our salvation, as a witness of His truth (John 18:37). We bear witness to that truth when we keep and observe the words of Torah.

The Words of Torah are an entrance, an "unfolding" into the wonders of G-D's greatness. This word *patach* / פֶּתַח, in its simplest form meanings "opening." Here in v. 131 it refers to "revelation" and "enlightenment." Many commentators refer to this opening as the unfolding and revelation of the Word of GOD.

Just think, the more we study, the more is revealed to us. We gain an entrance into the depths of the greatness of GOD. And because His greatness IS beyond our understanding, we should live a life continually seeking a deeper opening of our understanding. Open your mouth and receive a deeper understanding of the Word of GOD.

DECLARE THESE WORDS TODAY: *Open-Mouth Worship! 12 Omer Days Left! Expectation! Shavuot!*

Notes / Prayers / Reflections / Revelations

_____

_____

_____

_____

38 – COUNTING THE OMER פ

"Today is Day 38, which is 5 Weeks and 3 Days of the Omer."

Turn to me and be gracious to me, as is fitting to those who love Your Name. Direct my footsteps in Your word, and let no iniquity get mastery over me (132-133).

    In yesterday's devotional, we envisioned the letter *pe* (פ) as our mouths, wide open, hungry for, and in awe of G-D's wonders. The *pe* (פ) also shows us an open mouth that speaks. Today let's visualize the Word of G-D as an open mouth speaking to us. Let's also see the psalmist's wide open mouth crying out to G-D and attend to what this open mouth will teach us.

    Here the psalmist's open mouth is begging GOD to face him. The Hebrew literally says, "Face me, turn to me." When we say to someone, "Look at me," we are usually asking for attention. As a mother, I can remember and still often hear the cry of my children requesting my attention. "Mom, Mom, look what I can do. Mom, Mom, look, look."

    This cry for attention does not go away if I do not physically turn to them and attend to their needs. It may not even be a "real" need, but to them it is a need that requires attending to, not just looking toward. It requires a response and a reaction.

    This is the cry of the Psalmist, "Lord, attend to me with Your mercy." This should be the daily cry of our hearts. See and hear the open mouth of the Word of G-D and turn to attend to it. Open your mouth wide and cry to the Lord to attend to you with His mercy — not because you deserve it, but because it's who G-D is. The Psalmist makes his requests with an understanding of who G-D is and an understanding of his own shortcomings.

The following phrase, *"as is fitting..."* refers to G-D's judgment and declares a statement of His character, merciful in judgment. See the open mouth of the Word and hear G-D proclaim this about Himself: *"The LORD, the LORD God, is compassionate and gracious, slow to anger, abounding in loving devotion and faithfulness..."* (Exodus 34:6).

In verse 133 the Psalmist opens his mouth to speak another request for his footsteps to be established by the Word. He could have cried out for money or to be delivered or with some request driven by lustful desires. But his desire is that no iniquity would have dominion over him. This shows his dire need for G-D and his understanding of the bondage of sin. As G-D'S Word directs us, we can gain dominion over the sin in our lives, instead of allowing sin to have dominion over us. As long as we attend to the open mouth of the Word of G-D and open our mouths as well, as the Psalmist did!

DECLARE THESE WORDS TODAY: *My Mouth is Open! Face Me, LORD! Shavuot/Pentecost! 11 Days Left!*

Notes / Prayers / Reflections / Revelations

_____

_____

_____

_____

_____

_____

39 – COUNTING THE OMER פ

"Today is Day 39, which is 5 Weeks and 4 Days of the Omer."

Redeem me from human oppression, and I will keep Your precepts. Make Your face shine on Your servant, and teach me Your decrees. Streams of water run down from my eyes, because they do not observe Your Torah (134-136).

    Let's continue to look at two of the four requests the Psalmist made to GOD. The first request was made in verse 132: *"to be attended to with mercy."* The second request was made in verse 133: *"to be established by the Word."* I'm encouraging you this morning to open your mouth wide and make your request known, as King Xerxes said to Esther: *"What is Your desire?"* Open your mouth wide and ask, "inquire"/ *sh'al* / שאל of the Lord: make your desire, request made known just as the Psalmist is doing.

    This is the third request: *"Redeem me from the oppression of man, That I may keep Your precepts."* The Psalmist wanted freedom from oppression to properly obey Torah. Wow, I open my mouth in awe of this desire. I, too, desire to perfect my love for G-D by asking and making my desire known. **L-rd, G-D, I desire to be satisfied in You with every fraction of my heart, soul, might, and mind.** These requests were not selfish, but wise desires. They were driven by a heart of love for G-D and the things of G-D. It's a desire that cannot be attained by the things of this world. Too often we make requests of G-D for *things*. *Things* that we may not NEED, *things* that we see, *things* that can bring us into the entanglement of sin, *things* that fade away like the grass and our days. We are seeking the gifts and not the Giver. The Psalmist didn't say, *"Redeem me from the oppression of man so that I can get revenge or for any personal gain."* Our desire must be to keep G-D's precepts, to love who He is.

The fourth request was for an experience of G-D's greatness. Here the Psalmist uses the word *pa'necha* / פניך / *"Your face."* He is asking for G-D to shine upon him with favor and grace. I believe that when His face shines upon us, we begin to see how others have rejected Torah, but our response will not condemnation, but repentance: *"Streams of water run down from my eyes, because they do not observe Your Torah."* He was not just sorrowful over his own sins and iniquities, but he also deeply grieved because of the sins of others.

We should open our mouths wide like the *pe* (פ) and cry out to G-D for His mercy toward our loved ones. What desire of the heart are you seeking?

Open your mouth wide and speak that desire.

DECLARE THESE WORDS TODAY: *Open Mouth! Crying for Others! Counting Up! Shavuot! 16 Days!*

Notes / Prayers / Reflections / Revelations

_____

_____

_____

_____

_____

_____

40 – COUNTING THE OMER צ

"Today is Day 38, which is 5 Weeks and 3 Days of the Omer."

Righteous are You, Adonai, and Your judgments are upright. You have commanded righteousness, Your testimonies, and great faithfulness (137-139).

What better way to praise, honor, and extol our mighty GOD than to declare His attributes. In the stanza of Psalm 119, known by the Hebrew letter *tzadhe* (צ), the Psalmist declares a defining attribute of HaShem, i.e. His righteousness. He is all-together right and perfect; there is nothing or no one like Him. Whatever judgment He declares is a righteous judgment; there is no bending or swaying in what He judges (James 1:17). Isaiah asked these questions about Him: *"Who ... can instruct the LORD as His counselor; whom did He consult to enlighten Him; who taught Him the right way; who taught Him knowledge or showed Him understanding?"* (Isaiah 40:13-14).

All that proceeds from HaShem is righteous. When He gives us His commands, they are His Holy, righteous, and compassionate instructions given in order for us to have the opportunity to choose to be Holy as He is Holy (Leviticus 11:44). It is then that we can approach Him and worship Him in Spirit and in Truth (John 4:24). How we respond in worship is directly proportional to our obedience in following His Word and His commands. Conversely, to disregard attention and devotion to Hashem's Torah, to His Word, is akin to disregarding Him altogether! God forbid!

He knows our nature. He knows that unless He helps us, even with our best efforts, we will fail. David understands this when he says, *"My flesh and my heart may fail, but GOD is the strength of my heart and my portion forever"* (Psalm 73:26).

Blessed is He who comes in the Name of the Lord! The Father has made a way for us to approach Him through the perfect and Holy Sacrifice of Yeshua, our Mashiach who was actually more than a sacrifice. He was the *tzadik* (The Righteous One) whose death atones, not only for the nation of Israel, but also for the world. Now we can approach the Holiness of HaShem covered by His Son's perfect, atoning Blood (Hebrews 9:14).

ABBA, be merciful to us and grant us a heart devoted to Your Word, Your Commands, and Your Truths, B'Shem Yeshua! Amain.

Declare these words today: *Righteous Judgment! Yeshua! The Righteous One! Shavuot/Pentecost!*

Notes / Prayers / Reflections / Revelations

_____

_____

_____

_____

_____

_____

_____

_____

41 – COUNTING THE OMER צ

"Today is Day 41, which is 5 Weeks and 6 Days of the Omer."

Your word is thoroughly refined, and Your servant loves it. I am insignificant and despised, yet I have not forgotten Your precepts. Your justice is righteousness forever, and Your Torah is truth (140-142).

G-D's math is so different from the math we learned. When you consider how Gideon was called by G-D to go against the Midianites and the Amalekites at great odds of 1:675, you come to realize that one with G-D is always a majority. But these skewed mathematical odds did not just happen once. In fact, this is the way G-D demonstrates His power to His people, and to their enemies throughout biblical history, even to this day.

In Judges 7:2, HaShem told Gideon that He had to reduce his army; otherwise, Israel would glorify itself by saying that it was by their own strength that they defeated the enemy. We find a similar incident in II Chronicles 20. A great multitude was coming against King Jehoshaphat. Instead, as the Israelite worshippers began to sing and praise the LORD, He began to set ambushes against their enemies who were totally destroyed. And of course, don't forget the all-time favorite story of David and Goliath. Goliath, a great giant, came against a small, humble shepherd boy. We know the result; the great giant was taken down by the power of G-D and little David (1 Samuel 17).

In verse 141 the Psalmist says, *"I am insignificant and despised, yet I have not forgotten your precepts."* This

Psalmist was much like us when we face the giant of fear in our lives. We think of ourselves as insignificant and despised whenever the giants of fear confront us.

Fear will cause us to feel hopeless and powerless, but we cannot forget Adonai's precepts, His promises, and His presence when we put our trust in His Word. Like David, we need to confront our giants of fear in the same manner David spoke to the giant and said, *"You are coming to me with a sword, a spear and a javelin, but I am coming to you in the name of Adonai-Tzva'ot, God of the armies of Israel whom you have defied"* (I Samuel 17:45). By holding on to the precepts of Adonai, we will have the strength and courage to face any giant in our lives.

Perhaps you're facing giants of fear today that come from life's troubles. Remember, G-D's math is not like the math we learned. With His math, we can do anything through Messiah, who gives us strength (Philippians 4:13). Help us to see that greater is He who is in us than he who is in this world (I John 4:4b).

Be merciful to us, ABBA, as we put our trust in You. Amain.

DECLARE THESE WORDS TODAY: Different Math! Facing Giants! Shavuot/Pentecost!

Notes / Prayers / Reflections / Revelations

_____

_____

_____

_____

_____

_____

42 – COUNTING THE OMER צ

"Today is Day 42, which is 6 Weeks and 0 Days of the Omer."

Trouble and anguish have overtaken me, yet Your mitzvot are my delight. Your testimonies are righteous forever - make me understand, so I may live (143-144).

In the two verses above, the Psalmist concludes this section with the thought that G-D's character is unchanging (Psalm 55:19, Psalm 102:27). HaShem's standard of righteousness is reflected in His Word; this is the underlying theme of this section. How appropriate it is for the Psalmist to label this section (vv. 137-144) as *Tzade* (צ), which means "righteous." The "tzaddikim" are the "righteous ones" who stand with and for the unchanging Truths of HaShem. Anyone who stands for these unchanging truths will indeed experience anguish and trouble in this world. Yeshua warned us that in this life we will suffer persecution (John 16:33).

Hashem knows how difficult it is for us to sustain the continuous hardship of rejection, so He made a way for us to overcome and live victoriously. Yeshua suffered and died so that we can overcome (John 16:33b) *anything*. We can, therefore, take comfort and delight in His Truths. The Psalmist uses every means to illustrate His message to us. The website "Hebrews4Christians" describes it in this manner:

> The bent form of the letter *Tzade* (צ), represents righteous humility, but also is a picture of the suffering *Tzaddik*, which is also a picture of the LORD Yeshua

(as *Kiddushin* 406 states, 'suffering atones for sins.) The *sofit* [end] form of the letter (ץ) represents the elevated *Tzaddik*, standing up with arms lifted upward in victory and praise." The *Tzaddik* is none other than Yeshuah HaMashiach, whose suffering and death atoned for our sins.

If you ever feel overwhelmed with the many lies this world imposes on you, then take heart and know that only through Adonai's Word, can we have His unchanging Truth that will give us Yeshua's shalom, which cannot be obtained from the world. Remember, He warned us that if they hated Him, they will hate us, too (John 15:18). We're only temporary sojourners in this world, but the day will soon come when we will be eternally with Him.

Declare these words today: *RighteousTzdik! Counting Up! Shavuot/Pentecost! 7 Days Left!*

Notes / Prayers / Reflections / Revelations

_____

_____

_____

_____

_____

_____

_____

_____

_____

43 – COUNTING THE OMER ק

"Today is Day 43, which is 6 Weeks and 1 Days of the Omer."

I cried out with all my heart, 'Answer me, Adonai! I will keep Your decrees.' I cried out to You, 'Save me, and I will keep Your testimonies.' I am up before dawn, crying for help — I put my hope in Your word (145-146).

This section is introduced by the letter *koph* (ק) and begins with the word *ka'ra'ti* / קָרָאתִי. *"I cried"* (*kara'ti* / קָרָאתִי), the Psalmist says!

In these three verses, he uses *kara'ti* / קָרָאתִי three times. He cries for an **answer** ... for **salvation** ... for **help**!! Ever been there? I'm sure you have. You went to sleep crying and you woke up crying... and sometime throughout the day, you get the sense that even in your sleep you were crying.

When I visited the Holy Land, I saw the vast wilderness of Judea in southern Israel ... it's a desert ... rolling red hills for miles, but this is the terrain to which a fleeing David resided when he was trying to escape death at the hands of his enemies. It is a dry, empty and parched place. I saw the "supposed" cave of Adullam where David hid from Saul, and I could not help but experience his anguish. We never hear of accounts where David was rescued by his brothers or of how they came to his aid at any point in his life. After the fight with Goliath, we never hear of them again, which gives another aspect of David's plight. He was really alone!

Maybe that's how you feel! Alone! Maybe you are walking through a desert of grief right now, a wilderness of pain and disappointment. Maybe you feel as if you are in a cave; people see you, but they have no idea you are in an emotional or spiritual cave.

I love that David always gives the solution for every situation he is in. Want to hear his solutions? I know you do. Here they are:

I will **keep** Your **decrees**!
I will **keep** Your **testimonies**!
I **put** my **hope** in Your **Word!**

That's it, Beloved! That's it! The wildernesses of life are as sure as seedtime and harvest … but they are no surer than His Word. Get into it ... His decrees! Lose yourself in it .. His testimonies! Let it … His Word... get into you!! So that when you cry, your tears are effectual because they draw you closer to His Word, and therefore to Him! Maybe they will be tears like we experienced on Day 49!

May this word be written in every one of your tears… "HOPE."

DECLARE THESE WORDS TODAY: *Effectual Tears! Counting Up! Shavuot/Pentecost! HOPE!*

Notes / Prayers / Reflections / Revelations

_____
_____
_____
_____
_____
_____
_____
_____

44 – COUNTING THE OMER ק

"Today is Day 44, which is 6 Weeks and 2 Days of the Omer."

*My eyes are up before every night **watch**, as I meditate on Your word. Hear my voice with Your lovingkindness. Revive me, Adonai, with Your judgments (148-149).*

A few years ago, I remember a pastor telling me how he and his wife held evening sessions where she played her harp and sang while he integrated scripture and prayer into their times of worship and intercession. I told him that I was so blessed by that and wanted to do the same in my home. He said, "When you do it, that is a **watch**."

The pastor's response impacted me so much that my husband and I started a **watch** in our home; then another couple joined us my mom, my niece, a friend; and out of this grew the beginning of a worship team that we had no idea GOD was birthing ... all because we stood **watch**!

A **watch** is defined as "a period of vigil during which a person is stationed to look out for danger or trouble, typically during the night" *(Definitions from Oxford Languages)*. Having been on the battlefield, David knew the significance of a military **watch**; therefore, he understood the significance of a spiritual **watch**. You see, on the night **watch**, when everyone is asleep ... the enemy is not; he's up planning, scheming, even attacking. Before that critical "night **watch**," David's eyes were already open, so he grabbed the best defensive weapon against the enemy ... especially one who comes under the guise of night! The best defense? "Meditating or the Word."

It's not happenstance that Yeshua tells us to *"Keep watching und praying, so that you won't enter into temptation"* (Matthew 26:41).

"Watching" is being vigilant before the enemy attacks, and praying is your best defense and offense because, through prayer, the enemy is outsmarted, and his plans are foiled, and he is defeated.

When David kept vigilance in the night **watches**, he knew the result would be HaShem's responding to the voice of his meditation with lovingkindness. What was waiting for him beyond that was "revival," from the root *hayah* / היה which means everything from being alive to living prosperously.

On this 44th Day of Counting the Omer, as we steep ourselves in the reading of the Word, may we, too, discover the effectiveness of opening our eyes before "the night **watch**" and meditating on the Word so that it brings to us the Father's attention, and so that we are revived, not just with a charismatic wind, but also by being steeped in His judgments. That is living prosperously! That, my friend, is Revival!

DECLARE THESE WORDS TODAY: *The Night WATCH! Revival! Counting Up! 5 Days More!*

Notes / Prayers / Reflections / Revelations

_____

_____

_____

_____

_____

45 – COUNTING THE OMER ק

"Today is Day 45, which is 6 Weeks and 3 Days of the Omer."

Pursuers of wicked schemes draw near - they are far from Your Torah. You are near, Adonai, and all Your mitzvot are truth. Long ago learned from Your testimonies that You founded them firmly forever (150-152).

I love the juxtaposition that the Psalmist makes in verses 150-151. He says *"wicked schemes **draw near**,"* yet *"they are **far from Torah**"*!

And he says, *"You are near."* I would like to think that David is saying to G-D, "YOU are *nearer*!" Why? Because if you have the Torah, then HaShem is very close! He is within your heart, your mouth! For those who are wicked and are far from Torah, they have to deal with that which is closest to you! Can I get an Amen!? No matter how close their schemes get, they will get no closer to you than HaShem allows because He is ADONAI SHAMMAH - THE GOD WHO IS "THERE"!

David realizes something else as we see in v. 152. *"Long ago I learned from Your testimonies that You founded them firmly forever."* When did he learn that? When did he realize that the testimonies of GOD are forever fixed in the heavens. Maybe it was as a shepherd boy watching his father's sheep, and one night after herding them, he put them in their pens, took his harp and sat on a precipice somewhere in the mountains of Bethlehem in the region of Benjamin. He looked at the stars in their courses and the moon in its place. He remembered his Abba *Yishai* (Jesse) reading the Torah to him about how Elohim created the heavens and the earth!

In these instances, I believe, he pens Psalm 8:4 and says, *"When I consider Your heavens, the work of Your fingers, the moon and the stars, which You established.."* Maybe then he realized how GOD created each heavenly body with His metaphorical finger, told them to stay put, and they did! They were fixed, established, settled in the heavens! Why can't it also be with the Word of GOD which holds everything together? David believes it is! Do you?

Let's declare this to Wicked Schemes and Schemers: To get to me, you have to battle with Someone nearer to me than you! *HE* is THE ONE WHO FIRMLY FIXES HIS TESTIMONIES... FOREVER!

DECLARE THESE WORDS TODAY: *HalleluYah! Firmly Fixed! HE is NEAR! 5 Days More*!

Notes / Prayers / Reflections / Revelations

46 – COUNTING THE OMER ר

"Today is Day 46, which is 6 Weeks and 5 Days of the Omer."

See my affliction and rescue me, for I do not forget Your Torah. Defend my cause and redeem me. Restore my life through Your word. Salvation is far from the wicked, for they do not seek after Your decrees. Great are Your mercies, Adonai. Restore my life with Your judgments (153-156).

The 20th stanza begins with the 20th Hebrew letter *resh* (ר). Pictograms identify this Hebrew character as a person who is bent over with grief and pain. Others also describe this character as a symbol of humility, a bowing down, if you will, as a humble servant. (https://Chabad.org) A person can also see in this imagery the view of a humble servant, like Yeshua, who bows down toward us to meet us in our humility, afflictions, and difficulties.

You can almost feel the anguish of the Psalmist. He was desperate; the affliction must have been intense. But immediately afterwards, one can sense the sigh of relief when the psalmist received HaShem's Word. It is in HaShem's Words that this Psalmist was showered with mercies from above.

It would be hard for me to understand the feelings of this Psalmist if I had not experienced it firsthand. One frigid morning, many years ago, I barely had enough strength to get myself off the bed. You see, I was being treated for cancer with intense chemotherapy and radiation that made me feel the way the letter *resh* (ר) is described, stooped over, in intense weakness and pain. It was a humbling experience when I saw myself in the mirror; I saw a ghastly image. I was gaunt and pale, having lost over 100 pounds, and not having a single hair on my body. I struggled to find warmth in our home because it lacked heating. I managed to get myself enclosed in the kitchen and turned on the gas stove and oven to find some relief. It was then that I heard the words of Adonai say to my heart, 'My mercy and grace is new for you every morning." The relief was instant, because the intense discomfort was relieved by His intense love. Later, I found the words in Lamentation 3:21-26. I was also reminded of Paul's words when he heard the Lord say, *"My grace is sufficient for you"* (II Cor. 12:9).

Do you feel some form of anguish, pain, or distress today? You can certainly find His loving s*halom* in His words. Sometimes when we're in a state of despair and humility, and feeling so alone, He comes through by His Word that gives us joy unspeakable and full of glory (1Peter 1:8).

My friend, be strong and courageous (Joshua 1:9) because Adonai is with you. May the peace of Hashem be with you always! *Shalom Aleichem.*

DECLARE THESE WORDS TODAY: *His Grace Is Sufficient! The Resh! Shavuot! 3 More Days!*

Notes / Prayers / Reflections / Revelations

_____

_____

_____

_____

_____

_____

47 – COUNTING THE OMER ר

"Today is Day 47, which is 6 Weeks and 5 Days of the Omer."

Many are my persecutors and my toes. Yet I do not turn from Your testimonies. I see the treacherous and loathe them, because they do not keep Your word. See how I loved Your precepts. Restore my life, Adonai, with Your lovingkindness. Truth is the essence of Your word, and all Your righteous rulings are eternal (157-160).

There's a very lonely feeling when those, whom you have trusted and loved, turn against you. In those times, you feel a momentary sense of despair and abandonment. This type of abandonment is dark and lonely; no one in this world can give you relief. If you're not careful, you will begin to be filled with self-pity, which in turn, brings confusion and doubt, and ultimately leaves you faithless and filled with anger.

Unfortunately, when we experience betrayal and abandonment, we too quickly forget a most important Truth: HaShem will never leave us, nor forsake us (Deuteronomy 31:6-8). The letter *resh* (ר), which introduces this section as we learned in Day 45, can also mean the beginning or "the head of," as in the Hebrew word "rosh." Yeshua, who is our leader, our head, went before us and He experienced every possible abandonment imaginable; greater than anything we could possibly experience. He was abandoned by His followers, as He prophesied to Peter the night He was betrayed. When the rooster crowed three times all the disciples would forsake Him (Matthew 26:34).

However, the most extreme experience of abandonment was when He cried out from the cross, *"My GOD, My GOD, why have you forsaken me?"* (Luke 27:46). He knew all along that He had to die with all of our sins to atone for those sins before a Righteous GOD. He went ahead of us and paid our debt, all alone, because of His great love for us. He knew that we would not be able to pay for our own sins. He knew that we would be hopelessly and helplessly lost. Blessed be His glorious Name!

No doubt, like the psalmist, we sense disdain and we loathe those who callously profane His Name. Often I would tell my students when they carelessly fell into hasatan's traps, that by trespassing HaShem's word, they were nailing His hands back on the cross again; when they knowingly rejected Adonai's sacrifice, they were pressing harder on His crown of thorns; and, when they disregarded His love, they pierced His side, even to His heart.

If you feel alone and abandoned by those you love, remember that Yeshua went before you. He experienced abandonment, to the highest degree, and He still prays to the Father, *"Forgive them for they know not what they do"* (Luke 23:34). He goes as far as giving us His *Ruach* to comfort us, especially during times of abandonment.

Oh, ABBA, thank you for your love and grace for us that compelled You to go before us during our times of abandonment. Thank you for the gift of the *Ruach*, who comforts us in times like these, B'Shem Yeshua, Amain.

DECLARE THESE WORDS TODAY: *Comfort In Abandonment! Counting UP!*

Notes / Prayers / Reflections / Revelations

_____

_____

48 – COUNTING THE OMER ש

"Today is Day 47, which is Weeks and 6 Days of the Omer."

Princes persecute me for no reason, but my heart is in awe of Your words. I rejoice in Your word, as one who finds great spoil. I hate and abhor falsehood, but Your Torah I love. Seven times a day I praise You, because of Your righteous judgments. Great peace have they who love Your Torah, and nothing causes them to stumble (161-165).

We love to "sink our teeth" into the Word! Our leading letter for this section is *shin* (ש), meaning "tooth." Interestingly, the letter *shin* (ש) also symbolizes the Name G-D Almighty, El Shaddai / אל שדי which fulfills 2 Chronicles 6:6 topographically in that the letter *shin* (ש) can be seen in the valleys and hills of Jerusalem. *"But I have chosen Jerusalem that My Name would abide there and I have chosen David to be over My people Israel."* How detailed is the hand of Yeshua by which all things were made? How much are our hearts "in awe" of Him? This passage demonstrates how to be even more "awestruck."

King David, His chosen ruler, was certainly persecuted by princes, no doubt earthly and celestial principalities, as shown in Ephesians 6:2: *"For our struggle is not against flesh and blood, but against the rulers, against the powers, against the worldly forces of this darkness, and against the spiritual forces of wickedness in the heavenly places."* Who more than King David had to cling to Torah, truth, and WORSHIP? He worshipped seven times per day and in Psalms 34:2 even said, *"I will bless Adonai at all times. His praise is continually in my mouth."* As well, we are encouraged in Hebrews 13:15, *"Through Yeshua then, let us continually offer up to God a sacrifice of praise-the fruit of lips giving thanks to His name."* How important did the first earthly ruler of Jerusalem esteem worship? Do you think this played a part in why he was chosen?

When you think of the classic stories of explorers or pirates finding lost treasure, what is their reaction when the treasure is found? How would you react? King David rejoiced in HaShem's Word as, *"one who finds great spoil!?"* May the realization of the deep richness of the Word ever be alive in us and contagious! May it forever hold us in awe of His Greatness!

DECLARE THESE WORDS TODAY: *Awestruck! Finding Great Spoil! Counting UP! Shavuot!*

REFLECTION: The power given after we have stumbled was received by getting up, tracing back through the Word, and finding His peace again as one finding great treasure so to stumble no more!

Notes / Prayers / Reflections / Revelations

_____

_____

_____

_____

_____

_____

_____

49 – COUNTING THE OMER ש

"Today is Day 49, which is 7 Weeks and 0 Days of the Omer."

I hope for Your salvation, Adonai, and do Your mitzvot. My soul has observed Your testimonies and I love them exceedingly. I observe Your precepts and Your laws, for all my ways are before You (166-168).

As written, the letter *shin* (ש) can mean "that," "which," or "who." "What" or "Who" would be better to focus our attention on? Quick answer — there is no one greater to focus on than *El Shaddai* / אל שדי / G-D Almighty? This is Who King David hoped in for Salvation; and we do too.

Let's look more deeply at what "Salvation"/ישועה means, not only because of this hope and reliance, but also since the Psalmist bases this as a reference to doing HaShem's *mitzvot*. In fact, it is from the Name Yeshua / ישוע

Salvation / ישועה means "delivery, aid, victory, health, prosperity, safety and welfare." This is still the meaning from ancient times when King David wrote scripture by inspiration. Of course, today we know it includes the saving of our souls eternally, but David knew that is was only through HaShem was there power to save through immersion into His Word, precepts, and laws. This is how all His ways could be acceptable in G-D's sight.

What does it take to go from "observing" to "loving," as the Psalmist points out. Let's look at the word "observe" /שמר/ *shamar* = "properly to hedge about, guard, protect, attend to, beware, be circumspect, take heed, keep, mark, look narrowly, observe, preserve, regard, reserve, save, sure, wait for, watch(-man)." To apply these meanings to how we approach the Word takes a lot of time, attention and meditation, doesn't it?

Let's apply another big key - the depth of worship revealed in yesterday's passage. Imagine David applying the act of observing Adonai's testimonies fully as described here, precepts and laws and then enacting these concepts in worship!

To define "worship" /הלל/*hallel* = "to shine, to make a show, to boast, and thus be (clamorously) foolish, to race, to celebrate, commend, glory, give, sing, be worthy of praise, rage, renowned"... interesting. Romans 12:1 says, *"I urge you therefore, brothers and sisters, by the mercies of God, to present your bodies as a living sacrifice-holy, acceptable to God-which is your spiritual service."* "Service" is translated "worship" from the Greek.

And we are Watchmen! We've been given a great latitude in how we can worship, the key being that we observe WHO and present ourselves to WHOM? El Shaddai/ אל שדי/ Elohim Almighty, Almighty Adonai Who is the same yesterday, today and FOREVER!

DECLARE THESE WORDS TODAY: Happy 49th Day! Tomorrow —Shavuot/Pentecost!

Notes / Prayers / Reflections / Revelations

It's the 50th Day!!! ת

Let my cry come to You, Adonai. Grant me understanding by Your word. Let my supplication come before You. Deliver me, according to Your promise. My lips utter praise, for You teach me Your statutes. My tongue sings of Your word, for all Your mitzvot are righteous. Let Your hand be ready to help me, for I have chosen Your precepts. I long for Your deliverance, Adonai, and Your Torah is my delight. Let my soul live and praise you, and may Your rulings help me. I have strayed like a lost sheep- seek Your servant. For I did not forget Your mitzvot (169-176).

The *tav* (ת) is the last letter of the Hebrew alphabet. This passage begins with the word *tikrav* / תִּקְרַב, meaning to "draw near" as when the Psalmist says in verse 167, *"Let my cry come to You."* The *tav* (ת) in its Paleo Hebrew form looks like a T, some would say "a cross"! It is also a symbol of the *b'rit* / covenant. So it is not happenstance that the Psalmist, in the last part of Psalm 119, asks for several things: **#1** - he wants understanding, which is *bin* / בִּין one of the Spirits of G-D according to Isaiah 11. **#2** - He asks for deliverance. As believers, we know that deliverance doesn't mean that we are necessarily brought out of a situation, but that we are given the strength to endure that trial or test without profaning the Name of G-D! And if G-D brings us out - *Baruch HaShem*! Praise His Name! David, in the final declaration of this particular psalm, continues to ask the Lord to *"teach me Your chukkecha /* חֻקֶּיךָ */ Your statutes."* When He does, David declares that he will continue to sing the praises of GOD.

What a covenant that he continues to make with his lips as he does in Psalm 51:1-*"O Lord, open my lips, and my mouth will declare Your praise."* It is a covenant that says as the Lord continues to open David's mouth - that means every day with blessings of life and health — he will declare the praises of G-D.

Beloved, as we have left the days of the Counting of the Omer and now have reached Shavuot, I would encourage you to to make that covenant with your lips, your mouth, that as long as the Lord opens them, and teaches you His statutes, and has a ready hand to help, which He does, that you, too, would continue to praise Him.

Having been a shepherd of sheep and the Shepherd of Israel, David knew what it was like to corral a stray sheep. He felt he had become the same. On Shavuot, we get to commemorate *"matan Torah,"* the giving of Torah in Exodus 19-20, and the giving of the *Ruach* in Acts 2.

May we be like obedient sheep, never straying from the Commandments *(miztvot)*, Judgments *(mishpatim),* Testimonies *(edut/edot),* Statutes *(chukkim)* Precepts *(piqqudim), and* Word *(imrah)* of HaShem!

May our tongues, too, sing of His word, and may Torah always be our delight.

Chag Shavuot Sameach, Chaverim!

THE AUTHOR

Juanita Weiss is a retired English, journalism, and visual language teacher, having completed 30 years of exemplary service in the Virginia Beach City Public Schools. Juanita and her husband David founded Weiss Ministries, Inc., a 501(c)3 nonprofit ministry with a vision to bridge generational, denominational and cultural groups through the Jewish roots of the Christian faith. She has a MA in Communications from Regent University. Having studied and practiced Messianic Judaism for 36 years, Juanita completed a five-year program of study at Yeshivat Shuvu, an online Messianic Yeshiva, and received ordination as Morah Torah (Teacher of the Torah). An ordained minister with Evangelical Christian Alliance, Pastor Juanita Weiss serves in ministry with her husband Rabbi David at Malchut Chayim Messianic Congregation in Chesapeake, VA.

A WORD FROM THE AUTHOR TO THE CONTRIBUTORS

I am so blessed to be able to collaborate with amazing writers, some who did not even know they were writers. Thank you, Nia Cason; your writing is passionate and innocent. Thank you, Sarina Gilliland; your contributions are deep and meaningful; Thank you, Jackee Herndon; your writing is inspirational and fervent. Thank you, Jill Johnson; your writing is insightful and encouraging. Nelson Noriega; your writing is incisive and healing. Thank you, Carole; your writing is genuine and eye-opening. It has been such a pleasure to collaborate with you *all* in this publication that I know will bless others the way your contributions have blessed me. Thank you for taking this journey with me.

Check out our other Books on Amazon.com:
- *Clothed in Messiah: A Devotional for the 40 Days of Teshuvah from Elul to Yom Kippur*
- *Put OFF-Put ON: A Devotional for the Month of Elul*
- *49 Days - 49 Words: Counting the Omer through Psalm 67*
- *My Eyes See You: Reflections on the Book of Job*
- *The Trapped Messiah*
- *God STILL Uses Vessels*
- *Grains of Promise: The Beauty of Barley & Wheat, A Devotional*